ATLANTIC THRESHOLD

An oceanic and spiritual journey

Shirley Griffin.

Shirley shortly before setting sail on her Atlantic voyage in 1978

ATLANTIC THRESHOLD

An oceanic and spiritual journey

Shirley Ravenscroft Griffin

First edition 2008

Edited by William Bishop

ISBN 978-1-4092-0132-8

ATLANTIC THRESHOLD

A vigorous and poetic account of a single-handed sail across the Atlantic into the experience of an independent life.

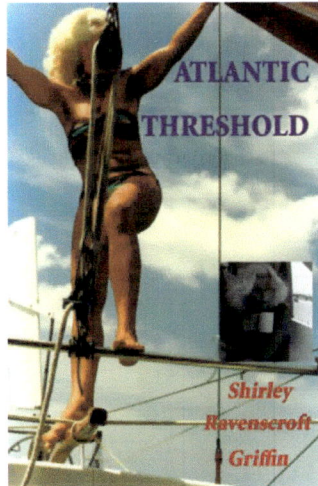

"Her book is at once a personal document, written primarily for herself and family, which we are privileged to share, and at the same time part of that ever growing canon of work where the courage to dare, to take on a challenge in one's life of epic proportions, is shared for others to find inspiration for their own trials and journeys. What sets this remarkble book apart from the normal telling of an adventure, is the, at times searing, honesty with which Shirley Griffin shares her inner thoughts and feelings."

Tom Raines, Edior - *New View*

Paperback 134pp £8.50

Order from your local bookshop: ISBN 978-1-4092-0132-8
or online at www.lulu.com/content/1488313

To Trevor who died peacefully in my arms on January 3rd 1989.

A most dear, controversial soul mate and companion on the long hard road, searching and finding the grail together as one, I dedicate this book with unending love and gratitude wherever you are. Without you, this most important experience of my lifetime could never have happened, the quest and dream remaining unfulfilled and my life incomplete.

Trevor Ravenscroft, December 1988

ACKNOWLEDGMENT

I am deeply conscious of the debt of gratitude I owe to the following who made my adventure possible and this book to be finally written, and most importantly of all, edited and published:

Captain Harry Harvey of Senner, Penzance, who took me under his wing in the 70's and taught me seamanship and coastal and celestial navigation in the Seamans Mission in Newlyn, Cornwall, giving me the confidence to accept the challenge of the single-handed crossing of the Atlantic in a small ill-equipped sail-boat.

The Dartmouth Valley U3A, started in the late 1990's.

Val Atkinson the convener of the writing group, and everyone in it who built up my confidence and ability to attempt to write. Carol Harding, the convener of a learners' group for individuals terrified of Word Processing.

David Harding, who has faithfully dealt with all the technical and functional difficulties arising with my word processor and work.

William Bishop, who has been a wonderful and supportive friend throughout: creative editor of the photographic magazine 'Inscape' who out of the kindness of his heart took on the laborious task of editing my work and facilitating its publication.

Virginia Khuri, for her loving and meaningful friendship, her valuable expertise and the sharing of her literary and academic skills.

CONTENTS

THE EXPLORERS by Martin Armstrong

We are the wandering souls that never rest:
No ancient loves can bind us, for the zest
And hunger of the eternal in us burn,
Driving us to adventure and to spurn
Ease and the humble joys within our ken
In the narrow earthly heavens of little men:-
Hunger for great experience, wisdom deep
Of nature and ourselves, those truths that leap
Flamelike to greet the faithful stress of soul
That forges on, seeking the glittering pole,
Through pain and terror and heart's agony
And many a windy battle on the sea.

Sunsets chaotic, fierce and beautiful
Fire the long furrow of our cleaving hull
And gild the coasts with wild and changing lights
Still ominous of elemental fights.
And the known coasts fall behind: the plunging ship
Leaps through untravelled seas. And, lo, the grip
About our hearts of a sudden and delighted fear
As the starry wonders glimmer and grow clear
Nightly, to nourish that unsated will
That goads us ever on to struggle still
On weltering decks in the roaring of ripped sails,
With maniac seas and screaming winds and the flails
Of lashing rain, in the clatter of hurled spray
Through nights moonless and starless, through long day
Of twilight windless till at evenfall
Thunder and lightening usher in the squall.

The loudest storms die down and cease to be,
But nourished by their strength and laughter we,
Unbeaten wrestlers, ever onward roll,
With warm, sea-freshened body and laughing soul,
Still eager for whatever shall befall;
And still, like lion-tamers, proudly call
New terrors and wonders forth from the unknown:
Gathering from toil and terrors overthrown,
From keen adventure and unabashed endeavour
The ambrosial food that keeps us young forever;
Seeking new worlds until our souls shall be
Wide as the frontiers of divinity.

8

GRAN SET FOR SOLO VOYAGE TO AMERICA

ON Friday afternoon 52-year-old grandmother Shirley Ravenscroft listened to the weather forecast, looked out at the mouth of the River Dart, effectively shuttered by a force nine gale, and knew it was not quite the time to sail the Atlantic single-handed.

Originally it was intended she would sail on September 21, but something has always cropped up something she has always wanted to do.

Her reason for setting sail at this time of year, when the gales are just beginning, is that her husband, five weeks ago, said, "You can have your boat to sail the Atlantic if you do it now." A lifetime of waiting was not going to be ruined by anything as mundane as gales.

The 26ft Contessa Teassa was seeing her son Raphael when she arrives in America.

Raphael is one of Britain and America's top saxophonists and has just brought out a long-playing record. "His dream is coming true and mine is about to. I hope we can meet up in America."

In the meantime her Dartmouth home at Gallants Bower will be waiting for her return.

ONE   Sailing from Dartmouth

When I awoke on that decisive morning in 1979, I could feel my boat, Teassa, tugging impatiently on her moorings to accommodate the outgoing tide of the River Dart. I scrambled from my bunk, dressed hurriedly and pulled a heavy weather jersey over my head as I clambered out on deck. A light rain had fallen during the night but the October sun was in the sky and the bright arc of a rainbow straddled the river entrance.

The moment had arrived to set off alone on a voyage across the Atlantic. I should have been overwhelmed with joy at the prospect of fulfilling the dream of a lifetime but instead I found myself in a terrifying state of panic and indecision. Everything looked distinctly different at that moment when I had to set sail and a brood of negative thoughts and self-doubts emerged from the deep recesses of my mind. If ever there was a moment when I was stripped of all resolve that was it. It seemed then to be no longer a beautiful scenario for unfulfilled dreams but a gale-ridden Hades of foam and spume.

If I really intended to go, then it was urgent that I left before the weather broke and November storms raged across the Western approaches and angry seas developed around Cape Finisterre. I had no more excuses. Everything was ready: every last piece of equipment had been obtained and all the electronic apparatus was installed, batteries charged, and food, water and fuel were aboard.

Though my peace of mind was completely shattered and my heart throbbed wildly, I somehow found the inner resolution to act. There was no time for procrastination. I therefore made a sudden decision to depart and climbed down into my Avon dinghy and, with trembling hands, arranged the warps on the mooring between the trots so that when I was ready I could slip free. I got back on deck and hauled the dinghy aboard, which was hard work for a woman only five feet tall. I deflated it and lashed it as compactly as possible between the life raft and the spray hood. The foresail, hanked onto the forestay and secured along the deck, and the main sail, loosely fastened with sail ties to the boom, were both ready to be easily released and raised. I therefore knelt in the cockpit and started the engine. Then I released the boat forward, and as the tide pulled her bow away from the trots, I freed her aft. With my heart in my mouth I pulled away and slowly edged Teassa through the lines of yachts and out into the river. This was it! It was the very first time that I had been alone and master of my own boat. My heart pounded with excitement.

As I passed the creek running below our whitewashed and green-shuttered cottage nestled among the trees, I triumphantly sounded my fog-horn to give a prearranged signal. My family was watching out for me and I could hear them! I had said my farewells the previous evening though. What joy I experienced at that moment when my lifelong dream was becoming reality with their support and encouragement.

"Gallants' Bower"

View of the estuary of the River Dart from Gallants' Bower

I left the engine to idle and put Teassa into the wind while I raised her proud red sails. With a touch of the tiller and the power of the tide, I fell off the wind, letting the sails fill. I then switched off the engine and we headed briskly for the mouth of the river. Then, as I approached the two rock promontories on either side of the river entrance, I had a feeling of déjà vu undoubtedly born out of some much earlier moment in time. For, in the manner of pictorial imagery in a dream, I recalled a childhood memory, around the age of eight. Though I was living far inland from the sea and had absolutely no knowledge of boats, I used to draw repetitively a tiny sailboat leaving a river entrance between two hillsides. I realized at that moment that it was a childhood precognition of the time of setting sail for the Atlantic and that I was fulfilling an episode in my life's destiny. Later, as I passed the castle, I could see figures waving madly from the cliffs above – it was my family.

Having cleared all obstacles, I set and adjusted the Hasler master self-steering gear for a course down channel. It was the first time that I had ever used it. It was amazingly simple and efficient however and worked perfectly. I had always wanted one of these self-steering contrivances and it was everything that I had hoped it would be and more besides. Trembling like a leaf in a blustery wind, I headed for the open sea and the adventure of a lifetime. What a sense of freedom I felt!

13

The mouth of River Dart

Though I was scared stiff, my heart was as happy as a skylark singing joyously to the sun on an early summer's day. It was an amazing experience to be alone like that, and to know that it was going to continue for weeks, even months ahead, especially after being surrounded by growing children and domestic responsibilities for twenty-six years without a break. I didn't even know what it was like to be alone for any length of time. Yet one thing I did know and that was that I was going to revel in it, for I was doing the one thing in the world that I had wanted to do for a very long time: sail an ocean all by myself and be absolutely free to make all my own decisions. It had about it the smell of paradise. Finally I was on my way to seek for that personal interaction in the vast lonely spaces of the ocean about which I had read so much but not known personally. I entertained the hope that I could become one with the sea that had wooed me over the years, ever calling in the depths of my mind and I felt greatly relieved to have escaped further intrusion and misrepresentation by the media into my very private affair: exploration of the soul in search of the spirit.

Certainly it might initially appear that fifty-two was ridiculously old for a woman on her own to confront the perils of the sea, but extensive reading about the history of single-handed sailing had revealed that most long voyages made by the earliest lone sailors had been achieved by people over fifty, and apparently that was not only because by then they had fulfilled their personal obligations and earned the money to buy their boats and had the leisure to set off on such an adventure. Rather it was because by then they had achieved a certain maturity of soul where such lone voyages offered the kind of challenging spiritual experiences without which their lives would no longer be meaningful.

One of the earliest voyagers, for example, was Brendon, an Irish monk who crossed the Atlantic fifteen hundred years ago. He is said to have set sail to rid himself of religious stagnation, subdue the flesh and implement his vow of poverty. That ancient monastic adventurer, who returned from North America with but a remnant of his crew, sought hardship not only as a stimulant to his religious devotions but in search of an elusive paradise within his own soul and mind. In modern times, no single-handers have either been so definitive, or so eloquent, regarding their motives for their self-chosen spells of solitude on the oceans of the world.

It was a beautiful day. The sun shone brightly over the blue dancing water and Teassa, rearing to begin, sailed eagerly westward down the coast in the arms of a friendly wind nursed easily by the self-steering gear. It gave me the opportunity to go below and extract my Walker Log from its box, with its impeller-cord tightly coiled. I took it up to the cockpit and placed it in a bracket on the stern and then tied the safety lanyard firmly to the back stay. Then I uncoiled the cord in order to stream it astern so that it would unwind, and then drew it back onto the boat, fitted its propeller, set the dials to zero and streamed the cord once more to set the first navigational reading of my voyage. That allowed me to record the sea miles sailed and therefore check on my snail-like progress across the ocean. I thought that it would be a delight to mark it up on the chart and it would also give me something to look forward to each day of the passage. I also took note of the course on the Sestral-More compass which was ridiculously large for my small boat and which I bought not only because of its reputation for accuracy but because it was so big and easy to read without glasses.

Noting the wind direction, I returned to the cabin, checked the tide and time, and made my first entry in the logbook. Then kneeling on the floor facing the portside bunk, I balanced myself on my elbows on the chart board suspended above the bunk like a desktop, and made my first tentative efforts to plot my position. I found it initially confusing because it was many years since I had attended navigation classes. So many things had happened in my life since then and I had forgotten more than I could remember. Fortunately I knew this part of the coast so well that it did not much matter. What was more important was that I would be able to practice using my unfamiliar radio direction finder while I sailed along the English coast towards the Atlantic and also be able to counter-check my position with the aid of radio beacons, because I had not used a sextant outside the classroom since 1971.

At that point I felt hungry so decided to have some stew which I had prepared the night before so that I would not need to cook on my first day out. I therefore heated it and served it into one of my free-gift Tupperware dishes and carried the steaming bowl up to the cockpit and sat down, wedging my feet on the opposite seat to keep my balance while I slowly consumed it. It was absolutely delicious. I had not realized how hungry I had become! Then I watched familiar landmarks falling slowly behind with the log spinning the first digits on the dial and indicating the first of thousands of sea miles that it would spin during the days ahead. What a tremendous relief it was to be on my way after the hectic weeks of preparation.

I began to recall the whole series of events through which I somehow prepared the yacht and it's equipment to sail before the weather conditions collapsed and prohibited such an enterprise as mine at that late time of the year.

Every morning I used to try to keep a personal tryst with my great love, the ocean. I lived in a seventeenth century cottage set high amidst the trees overlooking the River Dart which wound its steady way beside the ancient castle immediately below the cottage and out through the narrow channel to the sea. I always rose early and, on my way to the jagged point beside the river mouth, listened to the ocean tides breaking against the rocks – a rhythmical symphony of sound, which never failed to uplift my spirit. That early vigil became so much a habit for me that I felt like a lost soul all day if I failed to keep my morning rendezvous with the sunrise, which more often than not was the best part of the day. Each morning I followed the same winding paths through the woods before running across the sheep-cropped downs along trails gradually descending to the cliffs and then I turned back towards the river entrance. Many were the hidden vantage points sheltered from prevailing winds, offering unobstructed views of the ocean. Those were ideal places to contemplate the natural surroundings, meditate, or simply dream over and over again the one great aim of my life: to sail single-handed across the Atlantic. Little did I think, musing in the long grass on top of the cliff on that morning of a fateful day towards the end of August 1978, what a bombshell was going to hit me in the evening.

Gallants' Bower seen from below

My husband, Trevor, had recently arrived home from abroad with my older daughter, Michel, and her five-year-old daughter. In fact we had seen very little of each other for a year for he had been working as an aide to an Arab Prince.

I entered the sitting room to join the family after clearing up after supper and was dramatically confronted with the electrifying question: "If I buy you a boat and equip it with everything you think necessary, will you be prepared to sail the Atlantic in five weeks time?"

I was literally petrified. A stream of wild chaotic thoughts sped through my mind as the air hung in suspended silence waiting for my reply. I hadn't sailed for ten years. I had forgotten the navigation and I had never sailed alone, and certainly not in a keel boat. I had no idea how I would be able to prepare myself, let alone a boat which I hadn't even found –

and in five weeks. Yet after years of despair, I felt that this was my last chance. I knew that I was facing the critical turning point of my life. I had to make an irrevocable decision one way or another, for my decision would set the course of the remaining years of my life and I had to get it right. I knew that the fate-ridden answer had to be YES, for there might well never be such another opportunity. Most importantly, my daughter Michel was free to hold the fort which meant that Eve, my youngest daughter, would be cared for during my absence. My two other children, of course, had flown the nest.

YES I WILL was my definite and fear-filled reply, even though in my guts I sensed that there was some hidden agenda, as was usually the case with Trevor, which I would no doubt discover later to my cost.

In his determination to spur me into unaccustomed action, Trevor more or less threw me out of the cottage, and in hindsight I could see that it enabled Michel to take over all the responsibilities of the household without my interference. Fortunately also, I had the use of my much loved Volkswagen van until I had a boat to move onto, and I was left totally free – obviously a blessing in disguise.

I began my search with a frenzied scrutiny of the advertisements in the yachting magazines and made a number of fruitless journeys from which I returned slightly desolate and empty-handed. My hopes of finding a boat with a deep keel and an overall length that I would have the strength to handle alone were lessening by the day. I was also on unfamiliar ground as I was accustomed to multi-hulled boats. However, I had confidence in a sixth sense with regard to form and seaworthiness.

Eventually my efforts were rewarded and a week later I found 'Teassa' lying in a tiny creek up the River Dart, a little beyond the village of Dittisham. The gods were with me! A variety of thoughts passed through my mind while we viewed one another. I, standing in muddy water up to the top of my Wellington boots, she, settled aground and balanced on two sturdy legs, covered by a large orange tarpaulin slung over a strong mast which stretched over the bow from the stern. As I have said, I was accustomed to the spaciousness and the surfing performance of multi-hulls, and even though I was looking for a mono-hull like her, the extreme contrast had not reached me until that moment. She seemed desperately small, a bare twenty-six feet overall. I was instantly filled with apprehension at the unfamiliar angles of keel at which she would sail. But her lines pleased me well enough. You could have called it love at first sight!

Bringing Teassa down the River Dart from Dittisham in fog July 1978

She was a pretty lady, designed on the lines of a Norwegian folk boat, with a fiberglass-moulded pale blue-green hull relieved by white cabin sides and a deep rust coloured keel. She had a most pleasing swelling amidships and her rudder slanted sturdily down the stern of that deep and purposeful keel. I decided there and then that she would be mine.

A week later, with her keel repainted a racing copper, which I had accomplished between tides one sunny afternoon, the owner finally handed her over to me beside the floating dock in the river opposite Dartmouth Quay where a crane would step her mast.

Bringing Teassa down the River Dart from Dittisham in fog July 1978

Two weeks had passed and the pressure was on. The local boatyard had accepted the task of refitting her in time. Meanwhile I had to gather in the stores and, with the help of Trevor, drove up to London and to other places to find all the necessary pieces of equipment needed to be fitted. Just to name a few: new sets of red sails, self-steering gear, a marine radio and radio direction finder, sextant, barometer, chronometer, life raft, Avon dinghy, outboard engine, winches, safety harness, sheets and warps galore. It was the shopping spree of a lifetime!

After several days, I returned to the boatyard thinking that everything in the garden was lovely, namely that they were getting on with the refit, only to find the boatyard closed. The fair had arrived in town and the noise of generators was too much for the boatyard workers. I began to see that they hadn't taken me seriously at all, so I moved onto the boat in order that I could oversee every detail and galvanize the phlegmatic, laid-back, inefficient boatyard into action. It was one long misery until the night before my departure. It was no miracle that my project was brought together but the result of sheer brute determination born out of a commitment to the time element regarding the weather and the hope of finding the trade winds at their best. The only thing that I did not manage, and to my cost, was to have the engine fully overhauled or even renewed.

Teassa fitted out prior to the 1978/9 voyage

My reverie was broken as I became aware of the need to take evasive action to remove myself from the path of some fishing boats that were heading out from the coast. I was delighted with how easily Teassa responded to my needs and really began to enjoy sailing with her. I did become apprehensive though, for the day was drawing to a close. Newton Ferrers (close to Plymouth), which brought fond memories to mind, was not far distant to port. How inviting it seemed, but I knew that I had to resist its temptation and prepare for my first night alone at sea.

Newton Ferrers, a small village snuggled along the steep and beautiful wooded hillsides and shores of a charming river and estuary, was the perfect refuge for writers, artists and small sailing boats. I stayed there on two occasions. First of all with Trevor and my youngest daughter Eve, when Trevor had decided to begin writing his second book in 1973, and the second time when Eve and I escaped from living in a squat in London in 1976. Both stays were delightful short interludes in our lives between a year of travelling and sailing in North America, with a return to London.

I had made good headway westward throughout the day and familiarized myself with Teassa. She had virtually no overhangs, having a transom stern and a finely shaped bow section, so took very little pounding from the seas and took little or no water onboard, even when heeling over, because her ends were so light. The most vulnerable part of the boat was myself.

My mind was still in turmoil from the frantic weeks of getting her ready, and the naked fact was that I had only just begun to cross a huge expanse of sea, an ocean so large that the other side had at no reality for me then beyond the markings of an unfamiliar coastline on a piece of paper.

It became dark by six o'clock after the sun had set and I was desperately tired as my first night at sea closed in. Everything was new and unfamiliar and, because of the continuous motion of the boat and its heeling over, all jobs took an excessively long time to perform.

Two yachts ahead of me had slipped into Newton Ferrers, which I could see to starboard. I thought how blissful it would have been to be free from my aching body and the incessant motion, but I resisted, and as the wind was light, I went forward to exchange the large genoa sail for a smaller foresail, a gib which would be easier to handle if the weather changed in the night, though neither clouds nor the sea suggested it would.

The sail changes proved to be a bigger job than I had expected, especially folding the voluminous genoa into a very tiny sail bag and then lugging it the length of the boat into the cabin. I wedged it inside where it cluttered up the small interior but concentrated the weight amidships which could be crucial. I changed course and headed out to sea, crossing the shipping lanes while it was still light so that I could relax in comparative safety out of the way of the big ships. I planned to return close to the coast in the morning to make final checks on my radio direction-finder with radio beacons coming from as far as the Lizard Lighthouse from where I would sail west and then south to the Canary Islands.

I unearthed my shining new copper navigation lamps, which would help to conserve my batteries, and filled them with paraffin – no simple task in a rocking boat. Then I lit them and, balanced precariously on the cabin roof, hanked on by my safety harness, and fastened the lamps to their fittings on the stays. I looked all around while swaying to the gentle motion of the boat and clung onto the stays with my back pressed against the mast for support. There were no other boats anywhere. All I could see were the tiny lights of Plymouth receding into the darkness of the night.

The light wind in the sails gently drew Teassa away from dangers, but the waves looked very dark to my unaccustomed eyes and shocked me into remembrance that I was a very frightened person. Clambering back towards the cockpit, I checked that everything was in order on the deck and then climbed down the steps into the cabin and lit my brass paraffin cabin light, which had a gimbal attachment to allow it to swing to the motion of the boat and remain upright.

I switched on my radio to hear the shipping forecast and took the radio direction finder from its bracket to get cross-bearings on the various beacons in the area. Then I plotted my position on the chart, checked my compass bearing, and read off the log mileage.

I could only just stand upright in the centre of the cabin. Everything looked delightfully cosy with my soft feather sleeping bag and pillow lying invitingly on the starboard bunk. It had not turned cold but I wore a heavy sea jersey and the lined trousers of my yachting suit, which proved ideal for such circumstances. I cast my eyes around my small world with pleasure and satisfaction and could literally say that I had just about everything that I had ever dreamed of for a solo voyage across the ocean.

I heated some water in my kettle on the small two-ringed, gimbaled stove, made a hot drink of coffee and with the aid of pillows, propped myself against the cupboard underneath my radio. I sipped thoughtfully from my welcome drink as I prepared my mind for that first night at sea alone. I was carried backwards through the night on the wings of my sails, for my bunk faced the stern, and all I had to warn of my presence to any approaching vessel was my navigation lights and a radar reflector fixed high up in the stays.

I was so stiff and tired and groaned with pain as I tried to settle down more comfortably. My hands throbbed with nicks and soreness from handling the varied pieces of boating equipment and my whole body ached. However, I laid back and adjusted myself to the jerky and rocking motion of the boat. It was an eerie feeling to be in the unfamiliar aloneness and encompassing darkness. Teassa was doing well, sailing quite happily on her own with the combined help of the Hasler self-steering gear and the gentle south east wind filling her sails, drawing us forwards into the night.

Accompanying our passage through the water was a continuous symphony of sound which I hoped before long would become so familiar that even the smallest variation would entice me out on deck from any state of consciousness. On this occasion I listened with bated breath and beating heart, identifying the sounds of swishing, slapping, slushing water as it altered the pressure and tension on the fibre-glass hull of the boat which correspondingly strained the frames supporting it against the interior wood structures, causing strange creaks and groans from the bunks, fittings and engine casing.

It was to be a long weary night ahead since it took me a long while to learn to cat-nap. I decided to set the alarm clock so that I could sleep for half an hour, so fixed the sailcloth leeboard to the grab rail to prevent myself from falling from the bunk. I had hardly closed my eyes, so it seemed, when I had to claw my way out of a heavy blanket of sleep, roused by the ear-splitting noise of the alarm. My heart thumped like a terrified bird as I gathered my wits together. I stepped half way out of the cockpit as I clung to the edge of the cabin roof to look anxiously around for any approaching lights bearing down on me. There were none, thank God!

I settled back into my bunk again and set the alarm clock to repeat the performance. Once more I awoke in terror with the same unholy din in my ears after what seemed to have been only a matter of minutes. I squeezed my protesting body out of the cabin door. All was well. Teassa was rising and falling contentedly among the waves, her dark sails rhythmically swaying across the cloud-darkened sky, with the green starboard light and the red portside light shining brightly into the unbroken darkness. No vessels were in sight!

I decided that my nervous system could take no more of this. Anyway it was time to change course and to head towards land again and this meant eventually re-crossing the shipping lanes. Sleeping would then be like playing Russian Roulette! One thing was certain though, on the next day I would extricate myself from the situation I was in, weather permitting, and head out for the safety of the Atlantic.

We felt our way onto a new course. The steering gear was re-engaged and the log line once again trailed busily behind. I sat huddled in the cockpit behind a blue canvas windshield and my feet wedged me in tightly against the heel of the boat. I had never felt at home on the sea at night, and was certainly never at ease when a ghostly moon shone occasionally between clouds only to disappear again, leaving no visibility at all. Yet fortune was still with me because the wind had not risen and the seas were relatively quiet for the time of year.

To keep myself alert, I detached my faithful helmsman and took over the tiller for a spell. I could not be too careful when crossing shipping lanes. The foresail obscured my direct view ahead, so every now and then I made my way up to the bow to take a look for any ships that might be hidden behind the gib sail. I wondered how long it would take to become free from stiff joints and bruised muscles resulting from the continuous and unfamiliar movement of the boat and from sliding and blundering into unfamiliar objects both on deck and in the cabin. Later, while sitting huddled in the cockpit, feeling cold, wet and exhausted in the early hours of the morning, I listened to the sound of the sea and watched the rhythmical rise and fall of the bow of the yacht with the moon appearing and disappearing between clouds, and I was soothed into a sleepy reverie.

Like millions of other mothers, I had also experienced the tensions and conflicts between personal fulfilment and parental and domestic obligations. Yet I never sought for liberation in the sense of the Women's Liberation movement in which many women had been encouraged to see their homes as prisons and their children as their jailers. Perhaps such women will eventually discover that they are limited and confined by the very restrictions which they carry around with them, and that they were, in fact, their own jailers.

Before I married, I worked for five years as an unpaid teacher of handicapped children. I was interested above all else in supporting the rights of such children to have a full education under normal living conditions instead of being shut away in mental institutions where nothing was done to help them. I soon realized, as a comparatively young person, that freedom was in reality an inner question, a search for a quality of soul-life that could never be arranged but only discovered and lived. My first teaching job was in an experimental community on the Deeside in Scotland in association with an international gathering of some seventy young people who were involved in one way or another in helping to take care of, teach and nurture, around two hundred children with every form of physical and mental handicap. My own task was teaching a full curriculum to a class of twenty-three children, a few of whom were the normal children of other staff members, but the majority of whom were children from institutions, suffering from various forms of handicap.

It was an inspiration, joy and wonder to see how those children appeared to improve day by day in leaps and bounds as the result of constant caring, love and attention and how, under my care, they responded to a Waldorf school curriculum, a new approach to education instituted by Dr. Rudolf Steiner, philosopher, scientist and educator (1861–1925), noted for originating the science of the spirit known as Anthroposophy, and a pioneer of genius in many fields of learning.

That was an immensely important and fulfilling period of my life, especially so because I could always call on the resident doctors, psychiatrists and therapists. I found it particularly invigorating because most of my associates were also involved in some kind of spiritual quest beyond the narrow forms and beliefs of denominational religion. Somehow we found the time to attend a seminar for curative education, meetings and discussions on metaphysical themes, and lectures, often enjoying lively conversations into the early hours.

That community, which predated Findhorn by two decades, eventually mushroomed into the Camphill movement, which has spread worldwide to become a leading influence in bringing a full education to children and adults in need of special care. I thought that this vocation would become a career of a lifetime. However fate completely changed my plans. They say that love is blind! When Trevor came on a short visit, we fell in love and I left my job to join him at the end of the school year. He had been working as a journalist in London and abroad but at that time found little satisfaction in day-to-day reporting and feature writing for national newspapers and magazines. He wanted to become a professional writer but knew that it would take many years of reading and hard work before he was capable of earning a living as an author, or even discover what he really wanted to write about.

As I arose out of my reverie, I observed that two big ships had slid up channel to my starboard and their light-festooned presence gave them the appearance of great floating cities. I had to pass to their stern and get across the lane as quickly as I could sail. I was very thankful to God that my first night at sea was almost at its end.

By six in the morning everything dripped with condensation and the only comfort was the distant flashing light of the Eddystone Lighthouse visible to starboard. The wind had dropped as we slowly drew away from the shipping lanes and moved towards the comparative security of the Cornish coast and a new day. I was then able to warm my hands on a hot mug of coffee and savour its delicious aroma. How thankful I was for the spray-hood on the cabin roof and the dobies (canvas sheets on either side of the cockpit) giving protection from the cold.

The night before, when I left Plymouth astern, I was reminded of my first encounter with the South West. On leaving school at eighteen I joined the Auxiliary Territorial Service and after basic training was sent to Camberley, where the then Princess Elizabeth did a similar course, and spent three months learning to drive and maintain heavy vehicles – three tonners and the like. That was prior to a posting abroad to Egypt for my final two years of service in the Moasca garrison near Ismalia beside Lake Timsa on the Suez Canal. I had been trained in Cairo to become a telephone operator, and it was not long before I discovered the Services' yacht clubs on the Bitter lakes and Timsa and seized the opportunity to learn to sail and race dinghies whenever I could in that incredible desert environment.

My teachers were German prisoners of war, one a naval and the other a merchant sea captain, according to which club I sailed in. I was the only woman competing and as British officers considered it beneath their dignity to sail in the same boat with a ranker in the much-scorned A.T.S., one of my charming and cultured teachers was allowed to assist me instead. I was given the opportunity to join the Army Swimming and Diving Olympic Team if I stayed on in the service, but I declined. Sometimes I wondered if that was a missed opportunity, as one does in hindsight, but something inside me definitely wanted to move on.

I have a strong affinity with and affection for Devon and Cornwall. I remember that the initially unfamiliar proximity of the sea and the elements thrilled and spoke to my soul in countless ways, for I had lived inland all my life on the borders of the flat fens of East Anglia. Cornwall on the other hand, being a narrow peninsular, was exposed on three sides to the sea. The delightful winding roads sheltered by hedges and trees, old harbours, fishing villages and dramatic and scenic coastlines inset with heavenly white and golden beaches, caressed and cajoled by green translucent waters, were like paradise to me. Roots in that part of the world stretch far back into history, and the mystical life of the Celts particularly sparked off my imagination. I will never forget the glorious soul-inspiring sunrises and sunsets on my pilgrimages by foot from Mousehole and Longrow to my courses of navigation with a handful of fisherman in Newlyn where we were instructed by a deeply loved, old retired sea captain, called Captain Harvey, who had sailed before the mast in his youth.

My thoughts hurriedly returned to the practicalities of manoeuvring Teassa though, so I wedged my mug in a safe place, played with the sails to get the best out of them that I could, and adjusted the steering gear accordingly. Everything seemed secure and in order. How I longed for the first light of morning to release me from the prison of the night! I was by then in such a state of general tiredness and tension, although the tension had eased somewhat since parting company with Dartmouth.

I was by no means sure of myself and knew that it would take time to adjust. I decided to continue on the course that I had taken until sunrise, so picked up the mug and returned to the cabin. I took off my wet gear and hung it by the door to dry. Then I noted the time, distance covered, and compass course in my log and relaxed on my bunk. I told myself that I had to try to unravel my muddled thought and chaotic memories.

I must have dozed off because I awoke with a jolt with the noise of the sails slatting against the stays and the sheets rattling on the deck. The wind had completely dropped, leaving Teassa at the mercy of the rise and fall of the waves. She wallowed uncomfortably, rocking miserably from side to side. And then the sun shone brilliantly from a welcoming blue sky through the doorway, heralding the new day. I wondered just how long I had been asleep, and leapt out of the bunk in a state of shock, fearing the worst. I took a frightened look from the doorway, casting my eyes all around the boat. It was all clear. There was no other craft in sight. I therefore returned thankfully to the cabin and sat on my bunk to recover. Pulling on my boots and heavy sweater I suddenly realized how hungry I had become. Starving in fact! The day before I had only had some stew, an apple, a few handfuls of nuts and raisins, and some tea and coffee.

I gave priority though to going out on deck and downing the sails, securing the sheets and pulling in the log. I left the steering to my unenthusiastic first-mate who also disliked the lack of wind. But I knew that he would inevitably do his best, being the most faithful mate you could possibly expect to find – my self-steering gear of course.

Balancing myself as best I could, I carefully pumped some water into my small kettle, wedged it so that it could not skate around the stove, and lit a gas ring. A hot coffee was the first order of the day. I was also learning some hard lessons on how to cook in a small and volatile keel boat. I could not leave a single piece of equipment to its own devices, such as a spoon, mug or coffee jar. I only had one hand free to hold them however because my other hand was fully engaged in keeping my balance by grasping onto stable parts of the boat. I tended to lose the spoon under the stove, my knife on the floor, and spill the powdered milk when the boat lurched suddenly. I even had a fight on my hands keeping the coffee in the mug. Undaunted at that stage of my journey, I proceeded, in spite of madly swinging cupboard doors and having to burrow under a bunk-bed for provisions, to peel potatoes in sea water in a bucket, a move intended to save fresh water. After that I produced the most delicious breakfast of chips, egg, bacon and peas. The smell of the bacon out there at sea was incredible and absolutely mouth-watering!

That done, utensils and dishes washed up in my bucket of sea water and put away, I made the final preparations for my voyage such as stowing my anchor, warps and fenders, which I would not need until I made a landfall. I took down my navigation lights and cleaned and refilled them ready for the night ahead. It was then getting warmer and as I had the sea to myself, I stripped and had a wonderfully refreshing wash, changed my clothes, and then allowed myself to lay on my bunk and doze. I was absolutely exhausted. I knew that I was well out to sea, standing off the Cornish coast and outside the shipping lanes, so therefore reasonably safe.

I confess that I slept a whole blissful hour. It was 11.00 hours but I felt so much better for it. With no ships in view I had nothing to worry about, so I counted my blessings and resolved to relax since we were becalmed and were not going anywhere very speedily. The barometer had nothing much to say, registering neither a high nor a low, and there would be a shipping forecast on my radio eventually. I therefore propped up my uncomfortable body luxuriously on my bunk once more and, with a steaming hot cup of coffee, allowed a variety of thoughts and feelings to surface.

Eve at the age of ten

I missed Eve most terribly and experienced something akin to a deep pain within me. Eve was my youngest daughter aged ten, and a paradise child if there ever was one. She was the only one of the family that still needed me and I felt it within my being with all the intense feelings of motherhood. Yet I had to undertake the voyage for my own sake. After all, it was only a comparatively short time among all the lonely years in which we had resolutely stayed together however desperate things became, while the rest of the family members had spread their wings and sought their individual places in the world. I was merely beginning to spread mine, clumsily, hesitatingly, feeling the winds tentatively every day, not sure of their potentiality or strength, and awaiting the day when I could really fly.

Those conflicting feelings and thoughts in my soul made me remember how Trevor used to lament over his divided self and often quoted from Goethe's unique work 'Faust':

'Two, souls, Alas! Within my breast reside

And each repels the other!

One in tenacious lust the world

Holds in its embraces,

The other sweeps the dust above

Into the high ancestral places.'

We are conscious of those two contrasting selves within us but never more so than when we are alone. Indeed the Establishment knows the chastening effect of solitude and the worst legal punishment society can inflict on criminals is to lock them up alone for a spell, though never for more than thirty days at a time. In contrast, perpetual noise appears to be a barbiturate against the stark confrontation between those two aspects of ourselves, which when brought together, lead to a shattering sense of self-knowledge.

Having finished my coffee, I made the decision, due to the windless situation, to familiarize myself with my previously gained navigation skills. So, from the two shelves above each bunk, protected by netting to prevent books, navigational implements and miscellaneous items falling when the boat heeled over, I picked out the books that gave relevant information on tides and beacons such as lighthouses. It was initially all very confusing for me since I had to discover the Morse code signals beamed by the beacons and which group were in my direct vicinity, adjust the radio, put on the earphones, adjust the radio once more and concentrate sufficiently to catch what was, to begin with, a series of rapid Morse signals streaming from a host of sounds. Once the code from a particular beacon had been identified, I had to rotate the direction-finder from side to side until I could catch a null, which was the point where the

Trevor in 1979

signal from the beacon was least strong. I then read the bearing before repeating the whole process again on a number of other beacons to get cross bearings. Of course at the same time I had to keep my balance in that constantly moving environment. It really was not funny and my body was so painful from all the unaccustomed, continuous movement. I then noted my findings and applied them to my chart, checking the tide running under the boat and any possible leeway and then my compass bearing and log reading. I was very comforted by the results: the knowledge of my exact position.

I noticed that the barometer had been moving upwards almost imperceptibly and, on entering the cockpit, saw among other things a cargo ship steaming steadily up channel well to the south, and small clouds on the horizon and in addition tiny cat's paws on the surface of the sea, all of which were signs of wind. As it was midday, I sought out a tin of tomato soup from under my bunk, a saucepan from the sink cupboard, a tin-opener from the drawer above, and had a quick lunch.

I then put on another jersey and checked the bags of sails, spare sheets, warps and various stores and items in the bow, to make sure that they were all stowed well. I then switched on the engine in order to charge the batteries on which my radio depended. Then I headed towards the Lizard.

I could not believe the freedom that I felt. I had no home chores to do, no family to look after, beds to make, meals to cook or laundry or shopping to see to. All that needed was a bit of wind to help us past the Lizard and so finally be able to head for the open sea of the Atlantic.

Thinking about the Lizard, reminded me that 1971 marked the final completion of Trevor's first book, 'The Spear of Destiny', and a period of anxious waiting for its publication. We had found a lovely old thatched cottage for a winter let, appropriately named 'Hope Cottage', near Hope Cove near the end of the Lizard promontory. That beautiful Cornish coastline, bedecked with rare wild flowers, was a particular joy for Eve and for Candy our Labrador dog. Trevor, exhausted from his efforts in producing the book under trying circumstances, eventually recovered and helped to start a free newspaper called 'Peninsular West'. This was a new concept at the time. As for myself, I was loaned a van for the purpose of creating a fish-round on the Lizard. It enabled me to take Tristan, my younger son, to the prestigious Humphrey Davy Grammar School outside Penzance, and on my return journey to the Lizard, on certain days of the week, to collect fish in Newlyn, sell it, and return to Penzance in the afternoon to pick up Tristan.

The wind had found us at last. What a relief it was to switch off the engine and hear the end of its high-pitched whine. I lost no time in raising the main sail and witnessed the gentle wind fill the large genoa sail which reached back almost as far as the cockpit winches. I was delighted with the tan colour of the sails which added a picturesque touch to the boat with its light blue hull – and what a blessing that tan would prove to be when I sailed further south into the Atlantic where white sails would reflect the perpetual glare of the sun.

Some clouds scudded across the sky and because the wind was three quarters behind me, I went on a long reach out to sea, tacking in sharply before reaching out again, and so edged my way across the shipping lane south of the Lizard. How quickly the hours seemed to pass, accompanied by changing cloud patterns, which suggested to me mythological figures from old Celtic legends. I left my faithful helmsman steering the boat and prepared for nightfall.

Having cleared away supper while listening to the shipping forecast, I checked my position, but not without a fight with navigation tools: compass, dividers, parallel rulers, pencil and rubber all unmercifully skating around my makeshift navigation table. With the navigation lights set in the rigging, I put on warm clothes and, as the wind invariably altered during the evening, I exchanged the large genoa sail for a smaller gib, which would be easier to handle at night, and then went into the cabin to light my cabin lamp.

Everything was shipshape, but another dreaded night of catnapping lay ahead. I hoped that, with familiarity, my sleeping time would begin to lengthen as we freed ourselves from land and the shipping lanes, and I resolved that from then on I had to try to take more opportunities to rest during the daytime. Then, feeling more confident, I consoled myself with the thought that at least during the hours of darkness the visibility of my lights and the lights of passing shipping would provide some degree of navigational safety.

My watch told of the approach of midnight. Protected from the chill of the night by my heavy weather clothes, and wedged in the cockpit, I munched on a substantial mixture of nuts and raisins (an important stand-by on non-cooking occasions) and beat my way steadily down channel, wondering for better or worse, since I had recently become captain of my own ship, whether the experience of the voyage would give me the key to becoming master of my own soul as I had long dreamed that it could.

I certainly was not captain of my soul in my forties, and in reflecting on that lamentable fact I felt a deep sense of guilt and sorrow. It was difficult to face up to the memories of that period in family life which followed our arrival in the tiny Cornish fishing village of Mousehole, a small harbour nestling into the beautiful shore of Mounts Bay, which has been likened to the Bay of Naples by artists. It is also not far from the famous St. Michael's Mount, Penzance.

Up to that point it had been a reasonably good sail and we had advanced well over a hundred miles. I had only sighted four ships during the night and they were thankfully well to starboard. The wind had been flukey though, requiring two sail changes, and I eagerly awaited the new day in the hope that the sun would break over the far horizon in the east to warm me in my exhausted state. I would then have breakfast.

My voyage has been undertaken to provide me with a unique opportunity to stand aside from everyday life and take stock. It could possibly also involve a kind of death and rebirth. There can be no way of telling whether I would survive physically or mentally. Anyway this was the spice of adventure for me! I had at last given birth to a goal, long ago conceived, to place myself, unhampered by earthly obligations and physical restrictions, into the embrace of the elements that I felt so at home with and part of, and into the hands of the gods. I wanted to get as near to the spiritual world as I physically could and thereby closer to God. I wanted to arrive at a comprehension of my destiny; to know what I was doing in life and what course that I should take in the future. In fact I was in doubt about whether I actually had the freedom or the right to choose. I was unsure where the line was drawn between selfishness and attending to one's own needs, and unselfishness in relation to other human beings with their apparent needs. I understood from experiences I had as a curative teacher that if I reacted to a negative situation with a tough line of approach it could have a miraculous result. Then I felt like an onlooker. But with this voyage God was the one who looked and karma, which I had created myself, was to be my teacher.

I was so tired and frustrated at the controlling power of ignorance over my feelings and thoughts. Intuitions, urges, and impulses rose up continually, causing me to plunge in unknown and undreamt-of directions. It seemed to me that the body was the small boat that must be sailed single-handed by my individual human spirit across the stormy ocean of the soul to the land of the spirit. I had to navigate the appalling hazards caused by my inactive self in the contemporary material world.

Teassa made a good westing and there was nothing to worry about except that I was famished. I tried to do something about it but my body protested, aching all over. My will to action seemed to have slowed down. Time itself appeared different. There seemed to be no need to hurry. This was not helpful though, for I was in need of nourishment. I therefore slowly and painfully raised myself and went to my little kitchen (the galley) to make breakfast and start a new day.

THREE   Adjusting to Routines as Sea

I had been so busy sailing during the morning that when I entered the cabin, to check the time, I was surprised to discover that it was nearly noon. That was marvellous for it was lunch time and I was certainly ready for it.

In spite of many sail changes since the day before, I had great difficulty making a good westing. There had been no glorious sunshine to greet my morning, only a grey moody sea and sky and a changeable wind, and to my dismay I saw that the barometer was dropping. I was thankful though that I had taken the trouble to make a substantial breakfast in the early hours and taken a rest afterwards, because of being kept very busy working with the sails until midday. After I had checked my navigation procedures, I found that the beacons of the Scilly Isles and Finisterre gave me a good position.

Then I prepared a ship's stew, comprising potatoes from a sack in the bow and contents of miscellaneous tins, and took stock of my situation. It was my fourth day alone at sea and had been a good shakedown towards becoming familiar with my boat and acquiring skills in using my equipment and equating myself to a dot on a chart. I had begun to adjust my aching body to the endless punishment from the movement experienced in a small boat, and cope with the repeated setting and resetting of sails to accommodate changing winds – always hazardous on the small heaving deck – requiring bagging and de-bagging of sails and then lowering them through the fore-hatch and dragging them out again into the cockpit up onto the deck. That was awkward and heavy work by anyone's standards and scary at night.

I had in fact gradually learnt to develop a routine of procedures. First I clipped my safety harness to various vantage points such as the ratlines running from forward to aft. That ensured that any sudden movement of the boat, caused by an awkward wave motion, couldn't tip me over the railings into the sea when I moved out of the cockpit. Secondly, having edged along the narrow decking past the cabin sides to the bow and reclipped my harness, invariably a frustrating restriction to free movement, I would reach for the mast, loop one arm around it to steady my body and keep my balance, and release a sail halyard in order to drop a chosen sail. Thirdly, gathering the voluminous folds of the sail together, before the wind played havoc with it and blew it into the sea, I sat fair and square on the deck and carefully unclipped the halyard from the head of the sail and fastened it to the mast before it sailed away into the air and got caught in the rigging. Fourthly, with the sail stuffed in its bag, I detached the sheet and dropped the bag through the forward hatch, and so was ready to work on the replacement sail. All of this was accompanied by bangs and bruises everywhere and cuts and nicks to my hands, which the salt water and the grime from filling sooty lamps aggravated terribly. The last routine task of the day was putting the navigation lights into the rigging. It was an extremely dangerous operation in the half-light of evening, which on numerous occasions forced me to hang on for dear life.

After I had prepared my lunch, I carefully left the saucepan, with the remainder of the stew, wedged in the sink with its lid on and the sink's fitting cover over that. I was learning fast! Then I took my lunch out to the cockpit to eat. It was delicious, but I felt exhausted, and after finishing my stew, I put the bowl in a secured bucket ready for washing up, took an apple wrapped in tinfoil from the small hammock suspended from the cabin roof and returned to the cockpit. I sat dreamily watching Teassa's busy wake streaming behind us. It evoked a timeless state, but I had to be careful not to cling to a false sense of security which could descend on me through fatigue and familiarity, causing a mood which could stupefy my will!

Gazing balefully, in that kind of stupor, at the sullen sea, and fearfully at the grey sky, and uncomfortably at the lessening visibility, I decided to stir my bones. Teassa rattled her stays in disgust as I winched in the sheets to stop her sails flapping. No shipping was in sight and I wondered dubiously how long it would be before I was free from stiff joints and bruised and aching muscles caused by blundering into unfamiliar objects in the cabin and on deck. It was a vicious circle, I realized, as I took my protesting body down the steps into the cabin. My reflexes had slowed down in sympathy because every movement was uncomfortable and brought on more thumps and bumps.

Feeling tired, I propped myself up on the bunk and sipped thoughtfully at a steaming mug of coffee. Take that morning for instance where a great stretch of time had seemed only brief. Under normal circumstances when I wished for a mug of coffee, a simple task, I had in the first place to really want it – even desperately – because it was going to take an unusual amount of will and determination to make it, in view of the variety of physical deterrents. Even thinking about doing it could take a very long time indeed, because various factors were definitely opposed, like exhaustion, keeping one's balance in order to avoid being jerked unceremoniously against some unfortunate part of the boat because I hadn't a third or even fourth hand for support when the boat took a lurch. Equipment needed for the task was inclined to disappear under the stove or over it or on the floor, and there was always the chance of the coffee, that I had triumphantly made, being thrown out of the mug, with the attendant need to clear up the mess, and perhaps, after long consideration, if I was still sane by then, the decision to make another. How I missed the steady movement of our family's former trimaran, remembering how in a storm-ten the teapot that was left on the table was still there when it was all over.

During the morning I burnt my arm with boiling water. It felt like the last straw and it hurt! In fact I allowed myself to scream my head off with accumulated pain and frustration. I could do that when I was out on the ocean all by myself and I felt much better as a result!

One simple task, which could be completed in no time at all on shore, took considerably longer afloat. Indeed, when I was not particularly conscious of it, time would seem to quite happily slow down on its own. For example, during the night it was especially so. It took a Herculean effort to persuade myself to alter anything. Even Teassa protested at such a disturbance and rocked and plunged awkwardly through the wind and waves, shaking her sails in annoyance and tugging impatiently at the sheets which thumped noisily on the topsides which rattled the mainsheet block attached to the horse which reached over the tiller at the stern, which in turn worried the foresail tackle like a dog when I pushed hard on the tiller. It was an unholy and desperately alarming din at sea in the middle of the night when you were alone. I could see quite plainly the beginning of a process in which I would have a different experience of time.

I dozed for a while and it was three in the afternoon when I awoke. There were many things to do. I had to check for other craft, tend to Teassa, wash up, clean and fill the lamps and enter navigation data in my log. With that achieved, I topped up a bowl with nuts and fruit, of which I had a plentiful supply stored in large sweet jars, and took it out to the cockpit to munch at my leisure.

I was well content that I had got as far as I had, considering all the circumstances encountered on the way. I was in no hurry anyway. If I had been, I would have aimed to cross the Atlantic on a direct route to New York. Rather, I was heading naturally for the south like the birds, feeling my way toward the magical trade winds. From what I had read in books, sailing in them was akin to paradise for sailors such as myself. Indeed I was well aware when I accepted the challenge to attempt the voyage that winter weather would be following close at my heels and that I had to expect the possibility of consequences which could be dire.

I was deeply thankful though for the confidence and skills my old, nearly blind navigation teacher had given me. I could not have attempted the voyage without them. I remember Captain Harvey with a deep love and respect, with his infinite patience during lessons, laced with an outrageous humour and boundless expertise concerning seamanship. He made my life bearable at that time, and unknowingly facilitated the beginning of a serious personal search for my own identity during those unhappy years of living with the birth and completion of Trevor's first book. Neither could I have managed to attempt my voyage without the three years of experience gained in sailing and living on 'Highwayman' our trimaran. I thanked God that I had been so well taught by Captain Harvey to navigate by radio signals, for the sextant appeared not to be of much use, judging by the endless tracts of waves from horizon to horizon and the vast blanket of grey cloud overhead reaching as far as my eyes could see, leaving no possibility of taking a sight.

I knew some of the reasons why I was desperately uneasy about the Biscay, which I intended to avoid at all costs on my voyage. For a start the Bay was notorious for its capacity for diabolical weather conditions, throwing ships into distress. And significantly, when we, as a family, had intended to sail to Lisbon on Highwayman in 1966 on our way to New

Zealand, we had not only been becalmed, but were blown by heavy gales right into the southwest corner of the Bay, by which time, due to heavy seas, we had to spend three days repairing a broken steering-cable that controlled the rudder and we had also lost all engine power. It took a total of thirteen days to finally find an approachable northern Spanish harbour called Ribadeo. The journey was a nightmare right from the time when we left Guilvinec in Brittany.

With the eventual loss of Highwayman in 1969, through re-possession, together with the whole way of life that we had developed around it, and the shock of facing up to life on the dole in Mousehole, I was finally forced to question my own identity. All my own outside interests and possibilities seemed to have completely vanished. I questioned whether I was anything more than a wife and mother. I could not seem to find a rung to stand on which would also let me feel that I was an independent and developing individual with personal aims and interests reaching beyond the sphere of my family.

I was aware at the same time that both the masculine and feminine principle existed in every person and were not the exclusive attributes of either men or women. It was just those two contrasting aspects that I could not bring into harmony within myself. I was convinced that the individual human spirit in each person transcended the level of the sexes and could bring into harmony both the feminine and masculine qualities woven together in the soul-life of every person. But of course, I reasoned, the female or the male body must also affect how the spirit shines through: how we express ourselves, including the kind of experiences that confront us, and the way we deal with them. This kind of awareness should have allowed me to live out my differences as a woman without the feeling of being trapped and limited, but I still felt the need to develop within myself what women generally left the male to develop exclusively: those more purposeful, ambitious, outgoing traits that lead to outside accomplishments and fulfilment.

I didn't want to put on a masculine cloak and call it emancipation. I simply wanted to find some interest or occupation, alongside motherhood, which would challenge and complete the other side of my nature. I wanted to develop those other more positive, detached and objective aspects of myself involving intellect, will power and a capacity to achieve an individual purpose in the world. The whole world of navigation, with its ancient origins, history and science, had opened wide the door of my personal prison and allowed me to take my first steps on the expansive path of inner and outer exploration.

The night began to draw in and I needed to prepare for it. The wind was just adequate to allow passage in a southerly direction, so my prospects for pulling out any further into the Atlantic under those circumstances were negligible. I appeared to be totally alone in the world. I could see no shipping and wondered if I would be all right. I just did not want to get stuck once more in the Bay of Biscay. At least we were only at its mouth and so still had a fighting chance. All that I needed was a decent change of wind. I had to admit though, when I saw the barometer, that my prospects were poor. As a result I decided to cheer myself up by preparing my favourite meal of bacon, egg, chips and peas. But I realized that it was not going to be easy, so decided instead to have a hunk of my heavy Cranks wholemeal bread and dunk it in some soup.

I prepared the boat for the night and then prepared myself by pulling my waterproof trousers over my warm clothes. They drew up to my chest and were held up by braces. I certainly did not want a damp bottom from wet topsides. Then I took a satisfied look all around my little ship. Teassa had settled down, resigned to the poor winds, and was doing her best to make headway. I therefore huddled into the most comfortable position that I could find by the tiller and enjoyed a hot cup of tea.

Later, in the half-light of a partially hidden moon, when I wondered miserably once more the best way to deal with the sails, a beautiful event happened. It was one that I had never had the good fortune to experience before. Like an ethereal being from heaven, a tiny bird flew hesitantly onto Teassa's stern guardrail, which was rising and falling in sympathy with the sea. I could see that his tiny heartbeat pulsated quickly under the breast feathers. With his head cocked on one side in greeting, he hopped awkwardly towards a coil of rope, which hung from the bar along which the mainsail sheet-block ran, just behind my shoulder. Fluttering up into the air, the finch clutched the rope's end, shook and smoothed his feathers down, and without further ado, fell asleep.

I was so enchanted that I hardly dared to breathe for fear of creating a disturbance; in fact I was exceedingly comforted by this tiny creature. He must have been exhausted. The presence of another living being in the grey gloom of my watery wilderness for the first time since I had left Dartmouth nearly a week ago, made my heart fairly burst with joy! What a grace it was! I was passionately fond of birds and realize that the world would be a very empty place without them. I loved the heavenly symphony of joy welcoming the rising sun in the early hours of the morning for the benefit of the plants, trees and all living creatures and the very earth herself. The one would be impoverished without the other and nothing would be the same again. For me the gods, the beings living in the heavens, worked through such phenomena and my beleaguered soul was greatly comforted and helped with the visit of my tiny friend and messenger. I sat entranced for a long time and my heart filled with love.

Eventually, I crept as soundlessly as I was able down into the cabin, made tiny crumbs from a left over piece of crust, borrowed the lid from a jar, put water in it, and gingerly placed them on the stern for my guest. Fortunately there was nothing to change on deck at that point. Making note of the log and compass reading and wind direction, I went down below to prepare for sleep. I dozed on and off through the night, looking out from the cockpit at regular intervals and quietly adjusting sheets while tenderly looking to see if my friend was there.

Finally, in the early hours of the morning, I heard a sharp cry of pleasure as my tiny visitor soared up into the air past the mast, winging his way south. I felt an intense feeling of loneliness creeping over me though as the only tangible living creature that I had met since I had left home, disappeared into the sky.

FOUR   Becalmed and then Capsized by a Storm

As I prepared for my sixth day at sea, I realized that not only had my tiny friend flown away but that the wind had deserted me as well. We were completely and utterly becalmed. I therefore consoled myself by clearing up the deck in spite of the interminable rocking. After pulling the sails down and rolling them up and belaying them with their sheets along the deck so that they were easily accessible if needed, I took down the navigation lamps prior to cleaning and refilling, drew in the log's propeller, coiled its line and stowed it safely, and then prepared a tasty breakfast with a steaming hot cup of coffee to cheer myself up.

The day had become beautiful and hot even though it was October. So I festooned the rigging with washing and bedding. Despite the uncomfortable motion of my windless boat, I was having a great day. I took off all my clothes to enjoy it even better, for the ocean after all was literally all mine, and had a gloriously refreshing wash. By noon the boat and myself were as clean and bright and as orderly arranged as possible. Then after I had eaten a well-earned ship's stew, I sat daydreaming in the cockpit, mulling over the previous week in my mind.

I asked myself with passion why I had not learnt my lesson in 1966 about getting becalmed in the Biscay, and wondered if it was in fact possible for a person to learn all their lessons the first time around. It appeared that I had to admit to the simple fact that I had not got myself

45

sufficiently together in the first place. I simply did not have the time. So I was going to have to learn the hard way by making mistakes and facing up to things as they presented themselves and then think out solutions on the spot – hopefully!

This reflected my voyage through life. Frankly if I had personally sat down and worked it all out before I had started, I might never have got as far as being born. The simple fact was that I had not given the Bay a wide enough birth. Maybe that was because it was confusing for me, working on different charts that were not to the same scale. The charts were enormous in a small boat like mine and I had been working with the top arm of the Biscay with one chart and the bottom arm with another. There seemed to be masses of sea-room, but apparently it was all an illusion. I had not learnt to expand my imagination to encompass huge tracks of sea and work out the interaction between the land and the sea and the winds and the currents, and in this case the situation of the Bay in relationship to it all. Though, in self-defense, the winds had not permitted me to make a good westing.

The conclusion that I drew from these thoughts led to the beginning of an understanding of what was behind the extraordinary and inexplicable urge to undertake a lone voyage. I wanted to learn how to expand my whole being, to throw off the inhibitions and chains of my daily life, and to try to encompass the whole universe within my experience.

I suddenly became aware of a mast swaying across the heavens in the distance behind the beam, and coming in my direction. If it was a fellow human being in that vast empty expanse then I needed to put some clothes on. My spirits unexpectedly rose as my curiosity got the better of me. Here was a yacht under power, and a good sized one too. I used my binoculars to see better. The flag trailing at her stern told me she was French. If she came near I would be able to check my position.

As we wallowed and waited, I realized that she really was heading towards me, probably to check and see that I was all right. People care about one another on the sea, which was one of the reasons why I preferred life on water as opposed to living in a house.

Well in spite of the lack of French on my side and English on theirs, we managed, cheerily hailing each other as they slowly passed to starboard of me. They were satisfied that I was all right, and I was, with my position verified. With mixed feelings I gazed balefully after them, thinking how I would like to have a boat like that and look or rather be so professional, and with a splendid engine for getting out of that hell of the Biscay!

Feeling very sorry for myself, I pulled up a washboard from the floor of the cockpit and wedged it across the side seats. I then put my sleeping bag and pillow on top and fortified myself with a book and tried to stretch out as best I could. I just hoped that there was nothing that found my toes too interesting down below the surface since my feet were hanging over the edge of the boat.

I was absorbed in my book when the unbelievable happened. I felt something steadying itself on my head and on my knee. I looked down and it was an identical bird to my previous visitor. The one on my head flew onto the washboard at the bottom of my cabin entrance and I was absolutely spellbound. They were totally without fear and I felt transported into fairyland. I had approximately twelve visitors in the end but was never sure of their number as they explored the boat, flying in one end through the door of the cabin and out at the other – my forward hatch, which I had opened to air the boat thoroughly. They looked like finches and I watched entranced as they explored the boat, pushing under the netting that I had put in front of my shelves at the back of my bunks in order to prevent anything falling out when I was under sail, and disappearing under the sail bags in the bow. It was extraordinary how they appeared totally unafraid of my presence, as if I was part of their world rather than a great clumsy and insensitive human being to be avoided at all costs. I was hypnotized and time stood still!

Sad to say though, I did not realize what this interest was all about until a few days later because I became preoccupied with the arrival of another yacht to the south of me. I stood up to see further and quite unforgivably, in forgetting my tiny visitors, frightened them away. I was able to see an English flag on the stern of a very large twin-hulled catamaran. The crew had obviously decided to stay put for a while. It was irresistible. Without more ado I decided to up sticks. It provided a good excuse to charge my batteries by using the engine while at the same time going over to say hello. An hour later I found myself being helped aboard by three sets of strong welcoming arms and invited to dinner. What more could a lady ask in such circumstances!

Next morning, my seventh day at sea, I awoke after a wonderful fear-free night belayed to a long line astern of the cat. Then at sunrise I bade my hospitable sea-companions a grateful farewell as they freed Teassa. She turned her bow to receive a gentle wind to fill her sails, allowing her to draw slowly away. By 11.00 hours, with a tenuous and slow passage, helped by a north-west wind, we clawed our way out of the Biscay much to my relief.

The next day the barometer rose slowly and by nightfall the wind had moved north-eastward, which was perfect for my escape towards the Atlantic. As the wind was blowing force four to five, I was able to try out my twin poles with my largest genoa foresails for the first time. The only problem was that I was running only thirty miles off the Spanish coast not far from the part of the coast called Finisterre, well known for its undesirability if the weather turned nasty. But as they say, 'beggars can't be choosers'.

I was somewhat overwhelmed with my new task because I had never had the opportunity to use twin poles on a boat before. It was a superior piece of equipment, particularly useful for trade-wind sailing where the wind blew constantly from behind the boat. But quite honestly, fitting it was a ghastly job and took me the best part of two hours to set up. If there was ever a Granny in a tangle it was me with all the sheets, halyards, fittings, poles and sails plus my safety-harness clip which I had to attach to some place of safety at all times to avoid falling overboard. By the time that I had everything working to my satisfaction I was in a battered state. My hands hurt from being jagged on awkward fittings and my legs were bruised as I slid, on my knees, against various fittings protruding on the deck, due to the erratic movements of the boat.

After an hour though, everything had settled down, including my badly ruffled feathers. I was having the most splendid sail of the voyage up to that point. There were a number of sailing boats out enjoying the day as well, perhaps from the Spanish harbour of La Coruña.

During late afternoon I played for safety and reduced my sail area, replacing the genoas with my working sails, which were considerably smaller. I was not entirely happy about this though as I felt vulnerable in the dark with poles up and which you could not change in a hurry. However I wanted to take advantage of that favourable wind. As it turned out, I was kept very busy the whole night, but was rewarded with my first decent run of 78 miles. This was very satisfactory for my poor over-laden Teassa, and what was more, we were leaving Finisterre far astern!

We made very good headway on the following day, with big sails spread like wings flying over the deep blue, white-topped waves, scintillating and lovely in the golden sunshine. The wind force was five to six and I was as happy as a sand-boy. Teassa was like a great sea bird, with wings outspread and with her long straight keel showing me her paces. With her sea-kindly motion, this classically designed boat was born for a single-hander. I had to admit that on the one hand the speed was exciting yet on the other it was terrifying due to my lack of experience of deep water sailing in a keel-boat which lay low in the water in contrast to the trimaran which planed well over the surface.

We had been sailing well, but by noon the sea became lumpy and menacing in an unfamiliar way, with the wind gaining strength. It seemed too much for my little boat. Feeling distinctly uneasy and lacking in experience, I decided to take the poles down and reduce sail. It was a tricky business in that strange state of the sea. However with all the lines secured, unwieldy awkward poles clipped onto fittings on the deck, large foresails bagged and stowed in the bow, storm-sail hanked to the forestay and mainsail reefed down, we got back on course. With the violent motion of the boat stabilized, I began to make sure that she was ready for the worst by checking that everything was lashed down and secure. As it was mid-afternoon I prepared a quick snack and took it out to the cockpit. I did not like what I saw at all though. The movement of the boat was desperately uncomfortable, the sea looked ominous, and we were not making any headway despite the gale force seven wind.

I became afraid. There seemed no way around the situation but to heave-to. This was only something that I had read about in books and not something that I had ever experienced with our three-hulled trimaran, not even in a gale. So I placed my bare-poled craft head-on to the oncoming waves, made sure everything was battened down, and then went into the cabin and slatted up the doorway, except for the top washboard in order to have some ventilation. That was one of its advantages over a door.

I was deeply afraid and intimidated by the combination of the gale and enraged sea, and had an awful nagging and dragging feeling in my gut. I questioned whether I had done everything that it was possible to do, and kept thinking it over as I sat wedged on my bunk with my feet jammed hard against the opposite one, to counteract the infernal sea-sawing effect caused by the oncoming waves.

Every so often I heard a head of sea sloshing into the cockpit but that was dealt with by the self-draining system. My windows were boarded so that they would not stove in, and P.V.C. covers, which were set over the hatches, were secured by swing clamps, and the engine hatch was secured to the cabin sole with watertight joints. The marine batteries were lashed with shock cord and protected by a lid and the lower washboards were permanently fitted and packed with sealant. Sadly though, earlier in the voyage I had discovered that the plumbing from the sea-water inlet to the heads allowed salty water to find its way into the fresh water compartment, and so I had permanently turned them off so that no water could get in that way.

Teassa herself seemed to be all right and taking things in her stride, but because I was so utterly unfamiliar with keel boats, I cursed my ignorance. To keep my mind from my fears, I picked up my book on 'Heavy Weather Sailing' by Adlard Coles, an old yachtsman's Bible, and leafed through its pages. I wondered if there was anything in the book to compare to my circumstances, and if so what my alternatives were. My position certainly seemed to offer the least resistance to that strange sea, but there seemed to be a mysterious element. I wondered if it had to do with wind over tide and an ocean shelf beneath the sea where the sea meets a landmass. It did seem odd why the Biscay and Finisterre had such bad reputations. The very fact that our three yachts had converged on each other was not exactly to do with faulty navigation but rather with circumstances out of our control. But at that moment there was an earth-shattering crack above me!

Teassa was jerked from a roll to starboard, possibly by a freak wave pouring a huge weight of water onto the exposed keel, causing her to heel over dramatically to port. I felt myself falling backwards with the hull and remember crying out aloud in disbelief – Oh no! There was an unholy din as a cascade of objects, including cutlery, flew across the cabin. Then everything blacked out. It was only later that I learned that the earth-shattering crack, which I heard, was caused by the reversible load on the rigging.

I regained consciousness, slouched over the open bilges, surrounded by upended floorboards. My legs were in water nearly up to my knees and blood was flowing down from a gash over my left eye. It was a devastating mess! My instinct told me to check for damage on the deck above. Had I lost my mast, I wondered?

In spite of being in shock, I noticed that Teassa's movement was less violent. Trembling with fear, I carefully took down the slatted washboards one by one and climbed out into the cockpit. With shaking hands and wildly beating heart, I clutched onto the railings and looked around. It was unbelievable. I couldn't see any damage. My life raft and deflated-dinghy were safe and the rigging, which I had given so much thought and time to, was also completely intact.

This was the beginning of a deep love for my boat, Teassa, and the growth of a profound confidence in her abilities. One thing that I had learnt, though, was that I was not going to heave-to in a heavy sea again. It made me like a sitting duck waiting for extinction! If there were to be another occasion then we would take a different course of action. Little did I know then how vital this was to prove to be in the course of the voyage.

I was relieved to find that conditions soon began to change for the better. Returning to the cabin, I looked in a small mirror to see how bad my cut was. It could have done with a stitch or two but was not serious. I sat down and surveyed the scene. Judging by how the ingredients from the stew, originally covered by a lid, together with tea-leaves enclosed in a teapot covered by the sink lid, were spread more than half way around the cabin roof and in every nook and cranny imaginable, and also by the crazy angles at which the floorboards had come to rest, we must have rolled right over!

My bedding was a disaster. It was sopping wet, not only with water but also with ship's stew and tea-leaves. I wondered what I was going to do at night when it became cold. Fortunately however, I had spare clothes sealed in plastic bags. They were dry. So, gathering myself together, I bailed out the bilges, an awkward and dirty job at the best of times, dried and restored my tin cans and then put the floorboards back down. That made it easier to replace all the other items such as cutlery and cooking implements that were strewn about the cabin.

After peering into the inky darkness that night, I decided to leave things as they were until dawn and then to decide what course to take. It had been such a shock and I was once again absolutely exhausted. During the night I endeavored to sleep in all my clothes, heavy-weather gear included, and in addition I put a squeezed-out piece of bedding over myself to keep the warmth in. But still I was miserably cold.

When the next morning came, I was able to set a storm sail with a reefed-main and make passage southwards. I had decided that I would head for Lisbon in Portugal to get the boat checked over. My electrical equipment was faulty and the engine was not running well.

On the following day the gale blew itself out leaving me becalmed in fog, although just off the Portuguese coast, south of Lisbon. I was so close that I could hear the Atlantic rollers crashing onto the coast, but as

I had no wind or power I was at the mercy of the elements. It was a very uncomfortable and frightening position to be in yet again. I sat half-consciously in the cockpit, rocking incessantly from side to side like a baby in a cradle, and observed with a heavy heart the heaving grey-sea. Shutting my eyes, I prayed earnestly for some wind.

Later in the day I became conscious that Teassa's stays were covered in brightly coloured dragonflies, their wings shimmering with movement. I wondered if I had imagined it, but not so. It must have been due to the lack of movement in the air, which the dragonflies needed. I was hypnotized and was lost for words to describe such a wonder. I just felt an incredible warmth as if my heart was full of light. I could not remember them leaving later when a trickle of wind arose, allowing us to ghost towards Lisbon.

The next morning, with visibility still poor, the sun suddenly burst through the fog and drove away the night like a bad dream, drawing away the curtains of fog and revealing a glorious sight. Before my eyes lay the vast entrance to the great river that flowed towards Lisbon. It was guarded at its mouth by ancient fortresses built on the lonely promontories. It all seemed excitingly familiar as if I had been there before. The sun shone brilliantly on old white buildings set on a far distant shore. A deep resonating bell solemnly tolled its welcome. I was utterly overjoyed and felt totally at home.

Sample of press coverage at the time

Recovery after the storm

FIVE   Repairs and Time in Portugal

In the early hours of the morning, overjoyed and relieved to be free from the cold and impenetrable veils of fog and the deep fears caused by being incessantly becalmed, we were taken up by a steady tide and blown by a freshening wind right into the magnificent broad estuary of the famous River Tejo, one of Portugal's few natural harbours, used to inaugurate the 'Age of Discovery' in the 15th century. Its outstanding panoramic view of white town buildings, rising in terrace after terrace on a switchback of hills, was bathed in brilliant sunshine. It was like a dream! Everything was somehow familiar as if I had been there before.

The sun warmed the day and Teassa, picking up her skirts, heeled over to display her deep red keel to the cheers of sailors on a large vessel slipping past to starboard. I couldn't help blushing with pride for, after all, we were having a wonderful and exhilarating sail together. We literally flew up the river towards our first safe haven and I had to hold firmly onto the tiller. My heart rose with excitement and anticipation when I saw masts of yachts behind a wall on my port and a boat slipping into the hidden entrance. Further up river I saw the monument Padrao dos Descobrimentos, a memorial to Henry the Navigator, which jutted out from a high promontory. It was in the form of a huge stylized carvel boat made of limestone, with Prince Henry standing precariously on the bow ahead of his captains. Perhaps the knightly figure kneeling and holding Henry in a protective reverent embrace was the young Don Fransico Almeyda, who became the first Viceroy of India.

I doused my sails and had my warps, fenders, and boathook ready for any eventualities, and started up the engine ready to enter the harbour. While motoring round the wall, I saw an empty buoy over to the far left near to what looked like the Harbour Master's office. I hooked myself up to it and prepared to unleash and inflate my Avon dinghy so that I could go and find out where to berth Teassa. It was so marvellous to be safe, still, and at peace. But what a mess we were in!

I found the Harbour Master who could not have been more kind, helpful and friendly, and in what seemed no time at all, was shown a berth near the shore and secured Teassa by warps running from the bow and stern. Then I found the nearest telephone and rang my family. Michel my older daughter answered and was hugely excited to hear from me. I told her where I was, how things had been up to that point and that the Canary Islands would be my next destination, and I asked her to give my love to Eve whom I still missed dreadfully. With that I returned thankfully to the boat, made a cup of coffee and sat in the cockpit to relax. I was exhausted.

It was mid-afternoon, and while deciding on my next course of action, I became aware that a tall fair-haired English gentleman was hailing me from the shore. I wondered who it could possibly be as I climbed into my dinghy to go and meet him. It was the British Consul who had heard of my predicament. News certainly travelled fast so it seemed! He wanted to know if I was all right and if there was anything that he could do to help.

Through his intervention, I stayed in the Air Attaché's home until I was fit, shipshape, and ready to continue my voyage, which of course everyone found very intriguing and wanted to know all about. They were extremely charming and generous people who not only looked after me but allowed me to bring up all my fouled-up bedding and clothes and wash them in their washing machine and dry them outside. It was wonderful. It also enabled me to clean up the entire boat from the effects of capsizing and replenish stores, water, and fuel in preparation for leaving. I even found my reading glasses that I had been wearing at the time of capsizing and had lost. They were hiding under the engine.

At the end of my six-day stay, all those friendly people accompanied me to the harbour to bid me 'Bon Voyage'. I received a parting gift of a bottle of Vodka and was wished all the best. I thanked them profusely for their hospitality and rowed back to my boat, hauled the dinghy aboard, started the engine, detached the warps fore and aft and then pulled away, clearing the harbour ready for my sail down river towards the next leg of my voyage.

I stowed away all loose items, set the sails and steering gear, and made my way out to the mouth of the estuary. However what I had not known was that there was a violently agitated sea running across the entrance. I decided that I could not cope with that heaving turbulent sea which tossed the boat about unmercifully like a ping pong ball and also showered us with swirling water right over the deck for full measure. There must have been a terrific gale to cause such turbulence. So, after brief reflection, I decided to return to the safety of the yacht harbour. It was very frustrating, but all part of sailing life.

Eventually I drew up alongside a string of boats close to the entrance and away from the oil-covered warps near the shore. Helping hands assisted me to get alongside the end boat and fasten my lines to a large new wooden charter-yacht. I was invited aboard to tell my story and join in their evening meal. The owner said how he envied my little trouble-free Contessa, for he had once crossed the Atlantic on a solo voyage before he had built the present boat on which everything seemed to go wrong. Among other things his rudder had broken on the way down. We were indeed not the only ones to have had problems either, so he told me. This made me feel much better. Apparently there was a very capable Australian engineer aboard helping out, so after a couple of days, when it seemed all right, I gathered up my courage and asked him if, when he had a moment to spare, he would check out Teassa's electrics and engine for me.

Knights of the sea I call them all, and there were many, who so willingly gave me time, built up my confidence and gave a much appreciated comradeship, without all of which I would never have managed. We acted like a group of children, laughing and joking, and enjoying the adventure of entering Lisbon to seek spare parts for repairs and to experience Portugal, its people and food.

I loved the old-fashioned, ramshackle quality of the quarters that we saw, linked by a fascinating network of cobbled streets up whose outrageous gradients funiculars and cranked-trains climbed. I also delighted in the small shops in hidden away places, where we sought our bits and pieces, and the way the shopkeepers directed us from one shop to another in the most helpful and friendly fashion, even accompanying us to make certain that we arrived at the right shop. That could hardly be imagined in the society I was familiar with!

Eventually we discovered an incredibly palatial square with spectacular fountains, the like of which none of us had seen before and which stopped us in our tracks. It was simply magnificent!

As I have said before, time took on a different quality on a voyage. It took a long time to deal with tasks which otherwise could normally be dealt with quickly and it also required patience when entering a foreign harbour where you had no idea where to find what you needed and could not speak the language and knew no one. For me those days passed incredibly quickly, like windblown clouds scattering across the sky. The climate felt like an extended summer, encouraging the attitude that tomorrow was another day, so there was no reason to hurry.

At the end of the second week at Lisbon, my repairs were completed and the Harbour Master considered that the weather was satisfactory although, on reflection, he must have been considering it in relation to larger vessels. Anyway I decided to move on. Preparations for sailing always took a long time but finally I heaved up my dinghy, deflated it and lashed it down. Then when I looked up, I became aware of a tall man hurriedly sculling a dinghy towards me. He spoke in a deep, familiar guttural and broken English, strongly advising me not to set sail because he was familiar with these waters and knew that the weather in the Atlantic would become formidable over the next few days. He almost apologetically said that he hoped that I did not mind the warning. Then he turned his dinghy around and returned to his boat near the shore. Naturally I was disturbed at first but decided to take his advice.

To console myself, I recollected that Francis Drake, in 1577, waited two weeks for a favourable wind to set sail from Plymouth on his circumnavigation of the world, and then was blown back by gales and had to wait for another four weeks. I just had to be patient, so I reorganized things, pulling the sails down and re-stowing loose gear. After a hearty lunch, which I made at my leisure with no worry about some unexpected wave throwing me across the cabin, I decided to visit that gentleman and try to get to know him and discover more about the weather conditions.

I therefore rowed over to the old steel boat to which he had returned and I called out to see if anyone was home and whether I could come aboard to say hello. I wanted to thank him for his concern, for that was the least that I could do. My call was quickly answered and I was invited on board for a cup of coffee. He turned out to be a German doctor who had suffered heavy heart surgery and had escaped to sea on his boat to recover and write books. He showed me around. The boat was a combination of a very businesslike seagoing vessel and a writer's paradise with cabins lined with books and with a palatial combined study, navigation and cooking department. We got on very well for we had a lot of shared interests such as sailing and medicine and cultural interests. He told me about the boat and his aspirations and some things about his life, and I shared with him recollections of my early years in Camphill and asked if he was familiar with curative education based on Rudolf Steiner's thinking. He had heard of it but knew little about it, but nonetheless was interested to pursue the subject.

I tested him out with my thoughts concerning handicapped children to see how broad-minded he was, saying how the enigma of the handicapped child posed for me above all the question of the meaning of human destiny, and that if the materialistic view was correct, then the tragedy of such children appeared to be meaningless, accidental, hopeless and without a future and that if the materialistic view was carried to its logical extreme, all moral striving was but an empty convention as indeed it had become for large sections of the community.

He couldn't think of any other explanation apart from there being a heredity factor. I therefore proposed the idea of repeated earth-lives as a factor that rendered such lives meaningful, and asked him if he had ever considered that the Eastern conception of reincarnation and karma could somehow provide answers. Wasn't it, for example reasonable, I said, that what a person did in a single lifetime, whether acting in a creative or destructive manner towards people and the world, should have a result far wider and lasting than its immediate effect. Then realizing that what I had said could put an end to our conversation, I waited in silence. But he continued with our conversation, saying that he had heard of such thoughts but that his years of scientific training denied their probability. However he was interested in hearing me out for, from time to time, he had felt the need to ponder on the problems of handicapped patients and had never found any helpful answers.

I contributed the thought that it was common knowledge that the experiences of childhood had their effect throughout the whole life span, and persisted in unhealthy habits of living which led in later years to a diseased organism, and that surely it was possible for an unbiased mind to consider that defects that appeared at birth, or soon after in a handicapped child, could result from its actions in a previous life. I added that in my experience it was often the case that there was no proof of any heredity causes in the family history, but where there had been, the laws of karma themselves surely dictated that the child should be born into a body where the inherited conditions were present.

He sighed and said that he was afraid that was all too philosophical for him and that it was too late in life for him to change. But he admitted that what I had said gave him food for thought. He then needed to go ashore, but invited me to dinner for the following evening to continue our dialogue.

I whole-heartedly accepted the invitation and thanked him for his caring advice concerning the weather and his delicious mug of coffee and for showing me around his boat. Climbing down into my dinghy I waved farewell and rowed over to Teassa.

Next day I relaxed, read a book, slept, went exploring, and then cleaned up for my dinner-date and rowed over. As we ate supper together he commented that usually people on boats had nothing to say, but that I made a refreshing change. Then he told me about his writing project which involved charting all the rivers and harbours along the French coast inside the Biscay. I was suitably impressed. Then he told me about his family and how they visited him on his boat during his travels. He then proceeded to show me x-rays related to his heart operation and spoke about that. He had obviously been struggling with his condition and was very uncertain about his future.

I was keen to know if he knew anything about the background surrounding the life of Henry the Navigator, born in 1394, and what he thought about the so-called Age of Discovery. That was a subject close to my heart. Well he knew about it in a general way: that real exploration came about through Prince Henry, the third son of Joao and his English wife, Philippa, and that at the age of twenty six he became the Grand Master of the Order of Christ and turned the organization's vast resources towards marine development, founding a school of navigation at Sagres (literally regarded as the end of the world), and staffed it with Europe's leading cartographers, navigators and seamen. He also knew that as well as improving the art of off-shore navigation, Henry's staff redesigned the carvel, making it a vessel well suited to long ocean-going journeys, and as a result Madeira and the Azores were discovered in 1419 and 1427 respectively, and later, by the time of Henry's death in 1460, also the Cape Verde Islands plus the west coast of Africa to Sierra Leone. He also happened to know that through the treaty of Tordesillas in 1494, the two Iberian nations, Portugal and Spain, divided the world between them along an imaginary line 370 leagues west of the Cape Verde Islands, and by the mid 16th century dominated world trade.

It surprised me that, with his materialistic viewpoint and rejection of a spiritual foundation to life, he knew that Prince Henry was a Grand Master of the Order of Christ. But I was sure he would not have connected Prince Henry with the Knights Templar and the fact that the resources he spoke about were those of that disbanded Order which represented an international community of the Spirit. This is not generally known and also that individuals continue to search for the gold for which the Templars were persecuted, tortured and burnt to death. It was also unlikely that he knew that the inspiration for the opening up of the New World came from the great spiritually inspired Orders of Chivalry, all of which were cosmopolitan in character and intimately connected with the founding of the 'Order of the Knights of Santiago de Compostela', to which the creation of Portugal, as an independent nation, was related.

It was Philip the Fair-le-Bel of France, who with the help of the Pope, sought to completely annihilate the noble Knights Templar, but king Dinas of Portugal opposed it, and in order to preserve a nucleus of that powerful Order, he called in all its possessions and presented them to his newly founded 'Order of Christ'. In this way all the property of the Templars in Portugal and their statutes of chivalry, were preserved under another name along with their impulse towards an international community of the Spirit.

My fascination with the figure of Prince Henry began while I was studying navigation during the early 1970's, at the time when Trevor was struggling with his first book. I became conscious of the navigational problems of the medieval seafarer and those before them. I also became convinced then that the idea at that time of the world being flat, was not universally accepted. Indeed, in my twenties, during a time when I was teaching in Scotland, I had occasion to travel to Norway where I saw my first Viking ship, the 'Osberg', which was exhibited in Oslo. Its beauty of form and sublime craftsmanship spoke to the profoundest depths of my soul as if I were listening to an awe-inspiring symphony. In researching Viking history, my doubts increased and I came to believe that the Vikings explored the so-called New World before Columbus discovered it. For in order to become a Viking warrior, an individual had to prove their self capable of many skills, and it is possible that these voyages were employed to facilitate an initiatory effect on the soul-life. Indeed the impetus for my own voyage was inspired by a similar longing for this experience and desire for communion with the Spirit.

Before I left my host, he promised that he would tell me when the weather would be right to set sail. He estimated that it would be suitable after two or three days. As it happened I left on the fourth day. All the conditions were favourable and we sailed down the river with a fair wind on an ebbing tide, blessed with beautiful sunshine and all the warm thoughts of fellow sailors. My fears and apprehensions melted away as Teassa carried me swiftly and smoothly out of the river on a westerly tack, to clear the coast, ready to begin the next leg of my voyage southwards towards the Canary Islands. That would be my last port of call before crossing the Atlantic. With good fortune I should arrive there within ten days.

As the nautical miles sped under our keel, leaving a wake of silvery tresses streaming like day-dreams behind the stern in the Portuguese waters, I recalled those long past days in 1974 when Trevor decided to try to write his second book in a tiny Portuguese fishing village. Eve and I drove around in an old Volkswagon, exploring southern Portugal for three weeks. Quite by accident we discovered the magnificent Monastery of Batalha, with its structure built in the advanced Gothic style, revealing itself as a flamboyant construction of very great beauty. It had been in fact the most important artistic centre in Portugal in the fifteenth century. Inside we found the burial place of Joao, Philippa, and their four sons under an exquisitely carved star-studded dome. There was a statue of Prince Henry lying on his tomb, with the inscription 'Talant de Bien Fere'. How important that man had been in his lifetime and the difference he had made in the world is quite extraordinary!

Slowly we wound our way southwards towards the coast, wandering through the delightful wooded hills and rural countryside of southern Portugal, shopping in markets and villages set far back in time. We then spent glorious days by the sea exploring Lagos where Prince Henry had lived and worked and supervised shipbuilding. On our return journey we drove to the end of the medieval world, namely Sagres. It was at Sagres that Prince Henry built a nautical academy, an observatory, naval arsenal and a small town and fortress. Unfortunately very little has remained intact, but I was glad to experience the famous site and to stand on the windswept promontory surrounded by the vast and turbulent Atlantic ocean and to imagine how it must have been in Prince Henry's lifetime.

During the day, the wind was becoming westerly, about force four, but at night it invariably dropped and altered, causing many sail changes. I was therefore always kept very busy. At one time, after a restful sleep, I woke up to find the sails aback and sailing us in the wrong direction, which was very disconcerting. Of course having to tack all the time added hours and days to the voyage, but fortunately there were no more gales, fog or windless days. My only hazard was the occasional ship. One had tried to sneak up on my stern when I was engaged in navigation calculations, but fortunately I heard the sound of its engines throbbing through the water and rushed up in time to change my course to avoid a collision. There was no guarantee that a large ship could see your position or even had enough sea room to take avoiding action. At one time when I was cooking, an intuition caused me to down tools and leap into the cockpit. I was heading straight towards the middle of a passing ship. With my heart in my mouth, I switched on the engine, disconnected the steering gear, and with sheets and sails flapping frantically, steered Teassa clear. Fortunately we were all right and that was what mattered.

On the tenth day I approached the Canary Islands. Awakening from a rest, I climbed into the cockpit and saw that I was sailing towards two islands. From my pilot book, I identified them as the Grand Canary Island and the Island of Tenerife. I had originally wanted to go to the main island but on seeing the sun setting behind the volcanic mountain of Tenerife, a sight of incredible beauty, I decided to sail there.

SIX   Suicidal in Tenerife at Christmas

After leaving the coast of Portugal to stern, I had followed in the wake of the medieval Portuguese explorers on their southerly route into the unknown. Carried by the friendly Canary currents flowing past the African coast to our west, with the island of Madeira to the east, we slipped down between the Canary Islands. With night closing in, I ventured as close as I dared to the north western tip of the island of Tenerife. I watched the coastal lights until I could identify a harbour entrance and then stood off the coast until the early hours of the morning, for I did not have enough information or confidence to make my landfall in the dark. That gave me the opportunity to have a hearty meal, relax and prepare for an early start.

At 04.00 hours on my tenth day since leaving Lisbon, the sun was still abed as we set sail in the gloom. We ghosted cautiously on a light wind towards the main port of Santa Cruz. Guided by bright green and red lights flickering amidst a confusing array of city lights, I located the entrance to the port. Finally the sun rose in all its splendour behind me, lighting up a vast panoramic view of the port and its surroundings. I knew where I wanted to berth Teassa and so dowsed the sails and detached the steering gear in preparation. Then I helmed Teassa under power towards the end corner of the high outer harbour wall to my starboard. I was relieved to have arrived in the right position to guide Teassa around the wall so that I could get a temporary berth while making inquires where yachts could stay.

I tucked in, much to my amazement, behind a huge white, immaculately dressed sailing ship. On looking up at the flag, I realized that it was a magnificent Portuguese Tall Ship. It was absolutely spellbinding! Apparently someone aboard had seen me sailing from afar and had anticipated my needs and sent assistance in the form of a young sailor. He took my warps and belayed them to enormous bollards on the quayside while I checked my fenders. Then I hauled myself up an old rusty iron ladder between Teassa and the quayside, to reach the promenade. I gave thanks and then noticed that everything was covered in thick, black evil-smelling oil! It was absolutely foul stuff and incredibly difficult to avoid getting all over oneself and the boat topsides.

The young sailor had been instructed by the officer on watch to invite me aboard for a cup of coffee. I was pleasantly surprised and absolutely delighted. It was an offer that I couldn't refuse! Not only did it give me the unique opportunity to board the upper deck and see close-to-hand the soul-stirring rigging of the three-masted barque, which was breathtakingly beautiful, but it also enabled me to ask for advice. Thanking him, I accepted the gracious invitation and was led up the gangway onto the deck. I was overwhelmed by the size of the boat after life with Teassa. It was absolutely enormous. (It could have been 'Sagres II', distinguishable by the large red crosses on her sails, brought from Brazil in 1962.)

The smiling officer in charge of the early watch soon put me at my ease. He was very gallant. Intrigued to hear my story and to see if he could be of help, he sat me down with a large mug of steaming coffee. I could hardly believe my good fortune. My charming host told me that they were shortly embarking for a Tall Ships race. The full quota of personnel was aboard and within the hour they would be busy with last minute preparations for their voyage later in the day. It was very gracious of him to be so hospitable under such circumstances, but I guess it was not every day that a small suntanned, white-haired lady appeared from nowhere in the early hours of the morning in a small yacht and berthed under his stern.

On finishing the delicious coffee, and telling my tale, which impressed him, I thanked him profusely for his hospitality, and prepared to disembark. He had advised me to find a berth in the fishing harbour, which had ideal facilities for yachts. It was tucked away to the north of the extensive port with its own protective wall, so was out of the way of heavy shipping and had convenient access to the town and tax free ships' stores. With that useful information, I was soon under way heading for a more permanent berth across the immense harbour entrance.

I noticed the mast of a yacht in the distance disappearing in the direction I was intending taking and so I followed under sail. It was a sunny morning and I had a favourable wind and after about half an hour, looking to port, I saw an array of masts just visible in the distance, reaching above the high wall along the coast. But I could not see an entrance anywhere. However, looking through my binoculars, I was fortunate to just catch a glimpse of a small boat slipping past the rocky extremities of a concealed harbour entrance near the shore. It had obviously been positioned in that way to keep out heavy seas.

Arriving at a strange, unknown harbour from the ocean always worried me. Suddenly the sense of time altered and everything became urgent, even though all contingencies had been prepared for. So, I was under power, with my anchor and all my warps and fenders to hand. Teassa rose and sank, lurching dramatically as she crossed the heavy onshore surf. We cleared the outer harbour wall and surged thankfully into calm water. I saw a row of yachts lying abreast of each other ahead and steered for the outermost one. The owner saw me coming and welcomed me to my new berth. He helped me to tie up alongside him while I set the fenders. He said that if there was anything that I wanted to know I only had to ask. Thanking him for his kindness, I decided to tidy up all my loose gear lying around the deck and then sleep. I was tired-out.

By midday though I was refreshed but hungry. I decided to treat myself and go to find something to eat on shore. So I climbed carefully over side-rails and the bows and decks of an assortment of yachts to reach the quayside. I looked westwards over the rooftops of the town and could just see the jagged northern Anayla mountains with their rocky fangs reaching dramatically into the glorious blue sky. It was a highly dramatic backdrop to the capital.

Going ashore, I walked along the quay, which was set against the inside of the harbour wall, and then past a row of yachts moored alongside a pontoon. The architecture of the typically white Spanish buildings, with their shady trees and exotic flowers, created a welcoming, relaxed, holiday atmosphere. I found a cafe with a table outside sheltered by a gaily-coloured parasol, and wrote on my newly acquired postcards while waiting for lunch to arrive. A deep sense of contentment came over me as I lazily watched the world go by. It felt so absolutely perfect after a ten-day haul at sea.

It was not long before I heard English spoken at a nearby table. I thought that was most fortunate, so I completed my last postcard and went over to an elderly couple, apologized for disturbing their conversation, and asked them if they could tell me where I could get stamps for my cards and find a telephone, for I needed to ring home to England. They were kind and helpful and drew instructions on a piece of paper. Apparently they were on holiday and exploring the island by car and had just driven down from the mountains.

Ringing home was such a pleasure. Michel, my older daughter, was delighted to know that I had reached Tenerife and was safe. Eve was fine but longed for me to get back as quickly as possible. I said that I was going to have to spend time catching up on my celestial navigation, which I had forgotten. That entailed working through my old exercise books used during my navigation lessons in Cornwall ten years earlier. I had brought them along with me anticipating that I would have to do so. Also I needed further finance for I had to buy more stores and get the engine checked over, since it was faulty.

I returned to Teassa and sorted out my dirty clothes. It was wonderful to have the luxury of washing them in fresh water and hanging them out without fear of them being blown chaotically, or getting in the way of sails. With those chores out of the way, I scrubbed the decks with the remaining soapy water, cleared the windows, which were caked with salt, bagged my foresail and put on the main sail cover. I felt well satisfied with those efforts, so went inside to make a light supper and prepare for a night of luxury with absolutely nothing to worry about. By contrast with being at sea, this was heavenly.

During the next few days I became acquainted with my fellow yachtsmen. Several of them were preparing to cross the pond to various destinations. One was a delightful young single-hander Frenchman whose boat was taking on water and showed a definite list. Shortly before I left the harbour, he declared that he would gladly sail with me and help me with the navigation, since his boat was a write-off. Unfortunately though that would have negated everything that I was seeking. He was a skilled navigator too, but I had to disappoint him.

There were also three Americans who had to take a splendid yacht back to North America for its owner. We spent many happy hours together finding stores and exploring our environment. But calamity struck! Their boat sprang a leak and their time ran out and they had to return to America by air, leaving a sinking boat. Three enterprising young

Frenchmen, cramped together on their own small yacht close by, volunteered to keep the water level down by regular pumping while the owner was contacted. Eventually the desperate owner cut his losses and sold them the sinking yacht for a very low sum, which they raised, primarily with the sale of the engine in their own boat. I subsequently heard that they discovered that the cause of the intake of water was only a faulty valve. What good fortune for them!

After fruitless struggles with my old notes, I realized that I was in need of help with my celestial navigation. I simply could not understand the mathematics. My next door neighbour, who was returning to England next day, was equally puzzled but offered to introduce me to an American skipper and his wife who were living on a picturesque wooden yacht by the quay. He was sure they would be able to assist me. Well I met them later that day. They had just been cruising in the Mediterranean and were exploring the islands. The skipper was kindly and had the patience of Job, and I shall always remember him with deep gratitude. He concluded that the best course of action was to send for air-tables. They were much easier to use than the nautical tables. Meanwhile he would show me how to use his own and become familiar with my beautiful new sextant which had remained packed and unused in its box.

All these activities took time, but I hardly noticed how quickly the days passed because I was so constructively and happily occupied. Then there were always fellow adventurers to relax with, as for instance, when one day yachtsmen were challenged to a football match by sailors on a huge Russian factory trawler nearby. The sides were so uneven that the Russians gave our side some of their team. It was a hugely enjoyable game.

My air-tables and finances finally arrived and I was able to buy the remaining things that I needed for the last haul across the Atlantic. I had to carry a number of heavy two-gallon water containers for the water tank, and bottles of water as a back-up, and also petrol, paraffin, oil and an assortment of dry and fresh foods, all of which had to be located and laboriously carried by hand, and then manhandled over the neighbouring boats and finally stored. I examined the equipment on the boat and greased movable parts and then I searched through the rigging and sails for any signs of wear and tear, repairing wherever necessary. I was, by then, well acquainted with celestial navigation and as ready as I ever would be for the voyage, apart from the attention needed to the engine.

In the afternoon an English ex-transatlantic yachtsman hailed me from the quay. On holiday from Greece and accompanied by a girlfriend, he asked if he could take a look at my boat. After an animated conversation about boats, sailing, and all the pros and cons of my imminent voyage, he drew my attention to the fact that it was close to Christmas. I had totally forgotten all about it! Then he suggested that I sailed down to Christianos for Christmas before committing myself to the Atlantic crossing. Christianos was a charming small fishing harbour at the bottom of the island, only a short sail away, and a good launching point for my departure. There also seemed to be the possibility of a young engineer there who would be able to inspect the engine. Finally, he said that he would love to sail down there with me! His girlfriend would be able to drive their car down by road to meet us at the other end, and when we were ready they would both be delighted to take me on an exploration of the island and entertain me with dinner in their flat in the evening. I was most happy to fall in with their arrangements.

When we arrived the next day, we dropped Teassa's hook-like anchor in the small attractive outer harbour of Christianos, joining an assortment of yachts all facing out to sea. I inflated the Avon dinghy, lowered it into the water, and we climbed in and rowed ashore. We found his partner waiting in a nearby cafe and so sat down and made plans for our excursion the next day. The sail was enjoyable for him and gave me the opportunity to pick up all kinds of useful tips and information for my forthcoming venture.

The next day we drove towards Vilaflor, to the lower slopes of Mount Teida. It was breathtaking. In an hour and a half we had travelled from sea to snow, and from semi-desert to lava desert, and drove through areas of cool undulating pine forests, and into the badlands of Mt. Teida where burnt rubble lay scattered in terrifying abandonment like the surface of the moon. My friends told me that legend described that the Guanches, who were found living there when the island was discovered in the fourteenth century, believed that a devil lived in the bowels of the mountain and would one day rise and steal the sun. It hardly surprised me!

We drove to the east of Vilaflor where the road laboriously ascended the jagged crater walls that lined the southern side of a national park, where erosion of pyroclastic fragments had created an extraordinary moonscape of sandstone cones. We then snaked down into the interior crater called Las Canades. At one point we walked in the park so that we could explore the area, and found well camouflaged stone huts of the

Guanches, used long ago when sheep and goats were brought up to graze in the summer months. Apparently there was an intriguing notion that those native people, who were tall fair and blue-eyed, might have been Vikings. Indeed, they could well have been in view of the vagaries of the winds and ocean currents, and what was to me the deliberate lack of information concerning the voyages of the intrepid Vikings.

We discovered another enchanting theory, in literature for sale in a cafe on our route, when we decided to have a meal and relax. The suggestion was that the mountain ranges from the Azores, 1,300 miles south of Tenerife (which I would eventually sail past in Teassa), along with the Canaries and Madeira, were mountain ranges left over from Atlantis. That was a useful point of view to consider in my thoughtful exploration of the origins of Man.

On our return journey, my friends told me an interesting tale about Christopher Columbus who sailed passed Tenerife on his second voyage in 1492 when the volcano erupted, spewing vast quantities of glowing lava from its cone, hurling columns of swirling smoke and flames into the heavens. That frightening spectacle, accompanied by a deep and muffled roar in the earth's interior, caused a chronic state of panic among his sailors who believed that its cause was the undertaking of their voyage. That attitude very much fitted with the idea then held that the world was flat and that it was possible to fall off the edge into the fires of hell, or into some other unimaginable horror. I found that very significant because it related to a reason for undertaking my voyage, concerning the desire to explore my own state of consciousness and my self in relation to the world.

It had been a day of surprises, and when we found our way back to Christianos and had dinner together, I was deeply grateful to my hosts. Later that evening, we went down to the harbour to bid each other farewell. They wished me all the best for my voyage and then headed for home, leaving me to return to Teassa.

On December 25th, I gratefully accepted an invitation for lunch aboard a roomy English yacht, moored close by. The invitation came from two brothers, one accompanied by his wife, who were preparing to leave for the Caribbean islands for a holiday.

Christmas was quite an unreal concept for me at that time because of my preoccupation with the voyage. I had still been searching for someone to check Teasa's engine, and had been whiling away the time by intermittently diving into the cool pale green sea for relief from the hot sun, and generally exchanging stories of our experiences and general camaraderie with other yachtsmen. It was only later that evening, after a light meal, when I was really left to my own devices, that the reality of my situation came home to me. I decided to row ashore and attempt to walk the mood off. But everywhere there was the atmosphere and activity of Christmas festivities, which accentuated the painful fact that I was on my own. I returned in abject misery to Teassa.

It was the first time that I had not celebrated Christmas with Eve who meant so much to me. In the midst of preparing for the crossing, before I left home, I had not taken Christmas into account. I had been absent minded about the time of year, and had left absolutely nothing for her. I felt utterly dreadful! For I knew how much it meant to her and how abysmally selfish I had been. And to compound matters, I was assailed with this desperate and intense sense of loneliness. The dam broke. I just burst into irrepressible floods of tears, and waves of despair flooded over me. Behind it flowed an evil, dark, unbridled and overwhelming sense of fear, which rose like a monster from where it had been submerged, lurking in the dark depths of my subconscious mind waiting to break free. I was on a terrifying threshold about which I knew hardly anything. I was beside myself, and wondered what I could possibly do. Then I remembered that I had the bottle of vodka, which I had not wanted in the first place because my boat was a dry one. I decided to anaesthetize those uncontrollable feelings. I therefore searched for the bottle and found it at the back of the saucepan cupboard, unscrewed the top, and poured it into a mug and then sat on my bunk. It tasted horrible, but the acrid fumes hit the roof of my head and dulled my painful consciousness. I lay down on my bunk and tried to sleep but could not. So I drank some more and then went into the cockpit, throwing the rest overboard in disgust. I was then overcome by an uncontrollable urge to get into the dinghy and row out to sea.

I don't know how far I rowed before I became conscious of the sound of an outboard motor on the back of a dinghy and a comforting voice of a person calling out that it was far enough, and that he would take me home because tomorrow was another day. I was slowly towed by my dinghy warp back to Teassa and seen safely on board, and then bid goodnight. I lay down on my bunk like a sodden piece of driftwood, confused about who I was and with my thoughts circling round and round.

Who indeed was I? My childhood seemed like a fairy story where reality was hidden behind veils of dreamy self-awareness. I was a premature baby, born out of time, and I believed that it caused me to be a very slow developer and a perpetual dreamer. However I longed to make my dreams come true, and that was another reason why I was undertaking the voyage. It seemed to me that nothing about me had ever conformed. My outer circumstances ensured that it stayed that way. It wasn't a matter of despair, more of rejoicing, though I had to confess that at times things could seem like the end of the world – my own of course.

Shirley in front of the house in which she was brought up

The house in which I was brought up was originally an Elizabethan farmstead, surrounded by trees and covered in a profusion of flowers and fruit. It had retained its stables, paddock, meadows, gardens and orchard from earlier times. At one time it was isolated deep within the countryside but by the time that I was born it stood just within the outskirts of a small, sleepy market town built around a great Norman cathedral, once a pilgrimage centre equal to Rome, and the burial place of queens.

My father, a corn merchant, commuted to his office in the City by the London train and died of pneumonia when I was five years old. Unfortunately he had been unable to recover the loss of savings and investments in the business before I was born. As a result, my mother was slowly reduced to straitened circumstances. The servants left the house and my mother supported herself by taking in paying guests, assisted by my brother who was fifteen years older than myself (five other children had died in childbirth). He was forced to find work instead of staying at school.

Shirley at the age of five

A few years later a heart attack left my mother partially paralysed and she became increasingly unwell. Meanwhile, without a full measure of parental care, and missing my father more than I could tell, I ran wild in the flower-bedecked countryside, exploring the meadows, streams and woods, consoling myself in the arms of Mother Nature. I became passionately fond of animals, which abounded in those days. They became my closest friends in an otherwise unfriendly world. I also played out all kinds of childish adventures, stimulated by a vivid imagination related to the distant past and my immediate surroundings.

I must have been around ten years old when one day, without warning, a shadow was cast over my pagan dreams. My mother became a convert to the Catholic faith. Inevitably I became involved. I was too young to be able to question the new beliefs, which were thrust onto me, but I can remember how distressed I was to find that they did not embrace the universe of the sun, the moon, and the stars. The child in me could not understand a religion in which mother earth and all the kingdoms of nature were excluded. However I dutifully yet reluctantly attended lessons in the catechism and accompanied my mother to church, where I felt completely suffocated and wondered why it was that I felt nearer to God under the stars at night or when wandering through the beauty of the countryside on a summer's day. By the time that I reached puberty, my insatiable imagination had found new and Christian nourishment in all the wonderful stories about King Arthur and his Knights of the Round Table, and the quest for the Holy Grail.

Although Catholicism certainly contributed to the manner in which I sailed obliviously and sadly through adolescence without a single relationship with boys of my own age (home and school were strictly for girls, with dire penalties for those ever seen with a boy), I somehow compensated for this lack by living so fully in the history of the Age of Chivalry when the first buds of love emerged between the gallant knights and their ladies, especially between Tristan and Isolde, a story which I particularly cherished.

School meant little to me except the possibility of establishing my prowess in all physical activities, especially swimming and diving, gymnastics, tennis, hockey and netball. I loved acting in plays, and became the ultimate tomboy. I rode bareback on horses, which grazed in the fields, I climbed the highest forbidden trees and created rafts to sail on streams and ponds.

In later years I explored the castles, abbeys and cathedrals of England on my bicycle. Those buildings seemed to me like poems in stone. I was enchanted with their beauty, the grandeur of their proportions and the sense of peace and harmony that flowed from them. I stood in wonder beneath their bold vaulting, and absorbed their nobility of form, and bathed in the multicoloured light of the stained glass windows, somehow knowing intuitively that those magnificent buildings held secrets of a deep Christian knowledge that mankind had lost touch with. I had no idea about the secrets, or indeed that destiny would one day partially unveil them to me.

Sad to say, I had no sense for the meaning of personal destiny in those early days of my life. I could not perceive the preordained pattern of events or the web of personal relationships that could give a human life its unique form and meaning, so that the individual spirit within the soul could fulfil its tasks. All that I knew was that I was very much alone and would have to make my own way in the world without help of any kind. It was in that mood that I joined the A.T.S. not only to play my tiny part in the war then devastating Europe, but also to free myself from a home environment in which I had always been lacking in love, food and clothes. I reported to the training barracks in Hatfield still wearing my school skirt and blazer, and found myself entering another world.

For me the faculty of memory was quite mysterious. I found it odd how the pain, suffering, and causes of certain experiences, lay subconsciously buried while often only the fruitful and positive aspects rose to the surface, so that time often seemed negated. Take for instance the miraculous and instant recovery after carrying and giving birth to a baby. I had four under very hard circumstances. Indeed, my hidden self seemed to play subtle and evasive tactics, showing no desire for the light of consciousness to penetrate into the dark cave of memory.

SEVEN   From Canary Calm to Gale at Sea

I awoke early next day after a good night's sleep. In spite of feeling sheepish and confused about my evening's behaviour, I judged the cause to be excessive duress, and that allowed my sense of equanimity to return. Delighting in my restored mental state, I took a strip-down wash in wonderful hot fresh water, and put on clean clothes. Then I made coffee, filled a bowl with muesli, topped with my favourite soft, dark brown sugar and poured creamy milk onto it and sat down in the cockpit to enjoy my breakfast. It all helped fortify me to face another day.

I tidied up and prepared to go ashore. Armed with my reading glasses, an array of pencils, scissors, ruler and with my paper protected from the water in a plastic bag, I motored in my dinghy to the quayside and secured it to an iron ring, before climbing out onto the wall of the promenade. Following the promenade to its end, I had to step down onto a small stretch of golden sand and carefully pick my way across to the other side through an assortment of pink roasting torsos smeared in sickly-smelling oils and packed together like sardines. Reaching the other side, I sought out my favourite café not far from the harbour and sat down by a table. A strong coffee helped to fortify me.

The day was delightful, quiet and sun-filled as I set out my things on the table, resolving to create a small imaginative, illustrated booklet for Eve's birthday on January 20th. I decided that its contents would relate to my experiences after she waved goodbye to me from the distant cliff-tops of the River Dart in October. Resolving not to leave Tenerife until it was completed and safely posted, I started cutting and folding sheets of paper. The best way to tackle my project, I believed, was to use my encounters with natural life as a source of inspiration.

I thoroughly enjoyed the creative activity, and when I had completed my task in the following two days, I felt whole again. I then found an assortment of colourful postcards and wrote on them simple conversations that I had with the birds, bees and flowers concerning her, knowing that Eve, with her wonderful sense of imagination, would appreciate such small things. Like other children born with dyslexia, she also possessed a deeply imbued natural capacity for pure unconditional, open-hearted love, and would have no difficulty in understanding what I had to tell her. I missed her presence intensely.

Tenerife, January 1979. Wall damaged by storm.

On 30th December, after clearing up from a delicious breakfast of fresh eggs and Portuguese smoked bacon cut from a slab of rib hung from a rail which ran along the roof of the cabin above the galley, I heard a knock on the hull. I therefore climbed up to the cockpit and found that there was a young teenager standing there in a dinghy and hanging onto

Teassa's rails. He said that his father had sent him over to see if there was anything that he could do to get the engine running properly, adding that he was 'a dab hand' at engines.

That was a touch of grace, and caused me, in a flash, to survey my whole life and acknowledge that there really was a source, far wiser than my ordinary self, that looked after me, lending a steadying hand in the events in my life, enabling the ground plan to become established and fulfilled over time which I had carried unconsciously within my soul as I passed through the door of physical conception and birth.

I was delighted and hugely relieved at the young man's offer. He handed me what looked like a very professional bag of tools, and then belayed his dinghy and climbed aboard. He was apparently on holiday with his parents who were told of my dilemma by my friends before they moved on, and he came over as soon as he could free himself from the family Christmas celebrations. He explained that he intended to be an engineer when he grew up and really enjoyed any opportunity to apply his skills, especially since holidays could become very boring.

I told him there was something wrong with the gears and that the engine was losing power. He then became engrossed in the mysteries of Teasa's marine engine and proceeded to methodically search for faults. That engine was indeed the one item on the boat that I had not had the time to get overhauled before leaving Dartmouth. I wondered if the capsize might have caused its problems. Anyway, he did everything that he possibly could during short visits over two days, but he said that he could not fully identify the problem without the boat being taken out of the water. He agreed that it was possible that some seawater might have got into the system, as I had suspected. He said though that the engine was running better and that as I only needed to keep the batteries charged for receiving radio signals and using navigational lights at night during the rest of the voyage across the Atlantic, then I should be fine. I was intensely grateful to him for all his efforts, and said how good it was of him, and how I hoped that he would achieve his dream. His help restored my confidence.

I had wistfully watched yachts peel away from their moorings and slip away day by day, like migrating birds to their other destinations. Then, on New Year's Day, the last of the people that I knew left during the morning. I finally set off that afternoon, but not without mishap. I had totally forgotten that I had dropped the blade of my steering gear down the stern in order to protect it from passing boats in the harbour. This was because I had been busy with all the other preparations to leave, which included breaking my anchor free, dragging it aboard and then steering through numerous small craft which were out for the day.

I suddenly found that Teassa would not respond to the tiller as I put it down in order to head out to sea. Since I was then steering straight for a rocky shoreline I began to panic. Just in time, I realized what was wrong, and with shaking hands and pounding heart, I pulled the blade up and just cleared the rocks.

Tenerife, Canary Islands, January 1979

Leaving the harbour well astern, I then set the sails and headed south-westward in search of the famous trade winds. I felt a great relief in my soul after making the decision to let go of my last safe haven. I had the feeling that I had finally begun to sail into the realm where my hopes and dreams could be realized.

The east wind was fair, so I sailed on a broad reach in order to catch as much wind as I could. Leaving my mate in charge of the steering, I packed and stored all the things that I had needed for life ashore and prepared for the long haul.

After my midday lunch of mashed potatoes and mixed salad with tuna fish, followed by a sweet crunchy red apple for desert and a mug of coffee, I decided to put my feet up and have a good rest while I could. I was tired and realized that it was going to take time to readjust to the incessant movement and tasks of life afloat.

During the afternoon, I pulled myself sleepily from my bunk, put on the kettle and looked out. No boats were in sight and my faithful Teassa sailed as best she could in the light wind. Returning to the cabin, I made some tea and propped myself up in the bunk and thought over the recent days. The person who had pulled me back from a potential watery grave had gone ashore, but I was told that my friends with the car had asked him to keep a weather eye out for me because they knew that threshold fears existed to test everyone. I became very conscious of how indebted I was to so many fellow seafarers and fellow travellers in life, and my heart went out to them all wherever they were. I knew that I would remain grateful to them for the rest of my life.

As the day drew to a close, I pushed my feet into my deck shoes and put on a warm sweater. The irritable conversation between the sails and sheets indicated that they needed attention. But when I hoisted myself up to the cockpit, I became aware of the most spectacular and dramatic sunset that I had ever seen. The whole universe was a backcloth of bright rose-coloured hues, seared through with exploding colours of every kind, flooding the last remains of the fading blue sky of the day. Ominous black, elongated clouds in the mid-heavens, underlined with gleaming bands of gold, stretched from horizon to horizon and dark angry swirling clouds, shot through with deep malignant orange and reds, hung below. Pure startling white clouds, their edges etched by the light of the setting sun, boiled up from sea-level to the heights of the heavens, and the blood-red sun poised itself momentarily above the edge of the ocean.

My heart was filled with fear and apprehension, which then turned to wonder. The creative artist within my soul envisaged a vast panoramic picture emerging from the colours and forms of the clouds: a tableau depicting the lofty presence of the wise kings personifying the wisdom of the past ages, paying royal homage and sacrifice to the 'Holy Child' cradled in the heart of the sun. In astonishment, I wondered what kind of portent it could be. Then, as the imaginative scene dispersed and the fading colours merged into the grey of nightfall, I recalled that the Festival of the Three Kings on January 6th was close at hand. Then as night drew dark curtains over the drama of the evening, I felt deeply uneasy and sensed in my bones that all was not going to be well.

I adjusted the sails by winching in the sheets to harden the sails, placed the navigation lights in the rigging, and checked my steering gear. The wind was likely to be changeable as was its custom near a landmass. The loss of the warmth of the sun after sunset caused changes of temperature to both sea and land respectively and affected the air currents and wind direction. That demanded several changes of sails. Taking note of the mileage on the log and the compass reading, I went into the cabin and took radio bearings so that I could work out my position on the chart.

I knew that I was following the course the old windjammers sailed but which was no longer used by shipping, so I felt free from the incessant worry of large ships in my vicinity at night, and could relax without the need to keep a constant watch. I assumed that I would eventually have to change the sails, so I occupied myself by making a meal and relaxing on my bunk to enjoy it. I then contemplated the drama of the first day of my Atlantic crossing, particularly my experience at sunset. It reminded me that I had neglected to study and work consciously and meditatively through the weeks of Advent before Christmas. Indeed, I had been completely oblivious to the twelve holy nights! For it had been my custom and discipline throughout the cycle of each year to engage, through my inner life, with the festivals and their associated Christian Mysteries. They constituted approachable thresholds for me, where the heavenly came into contact with the earthly in an existential way. Indeed during the voyage, I had experienced within myself widely contrasting states of soul: the visual panoramic expansion of the self to the limits of the universe, and the deep contraction of the self into a tight centre of abject inner fear. I felt sure that had something to do with the thresholds of death and birth.

Teassa was absolutely miserable – unable to make way and ghosting along with a genoa sail flapping uselessly. I therefore put on my heavy weather gear, grabbed my torch and clambered out onto the deck. I took the genoa sail down and stored the spinnaker-pole that had been holding it out, hanked the working jib onto the forestay, tightened up the main sail, and took a starboard tack. When I returned to the cabin it was 20.00 hours, so I hung up my wet gear and took a last look at my barometer before getting into my sleeping bag. The barometer reading had dropped considerably. That meant that the air pressure was decreasing, indicating stormy weather. I felt apprehensive but could not countenance the idea of turning back and starting all over again, because my course was set. I would have to accept conditions as they arose.

Early next day, in spite of the wind dropping to force three in sympathy with my barometer, we still ran well with the help of the Canary current. The temperature was quite cold after the heat of Tenerife though, so I wore my heavy sweaters again. My first mate had a sure hand on the tiller and the log indicated that we had covered the first sixty miles of our approximately 2,700 mile voyage, and our compass course remained steady. I searched the sky for weather portents and noticed that the clouds in the sky looked as if scratched by a hen, indicating a possible gale ahead. That made me decide to have breakfast since it would help to keep my spirits up.

As I climbed down the steps into the cabin, I realized how important meals were to me, not only out of necessity but because they were something to look forward to on a regular basis whatever happened. There could be a festive quality to a meal. Indeed I had put a lot of thought into my food supplies before starting my voyage, for I had to cater for a long stretch of time. It made me realize how much I had taken food for granted and not put sufficient thought into nutritional values. I had also overlooked the importance of water. I could not just turn on my tap on board as liberally as at home. The amount that I could carry was limited, and the question had to be answered as to how many mugs of water I needed for drinking and cooking each day.

I made some porridge in an attempt to warm myself up, and cut off two hunks from one of my precious loaves; precious because they had a limited life, and then I would only have crackers and the like, since there was no shop conveniently around the corner. Sparingly, I spread butter and marmalade to make them last, filled a mug with hot coffee and ate and drank sitting on my bunk. The unfamiliar movement of the boat, after my spell on shore, forced me to be extremely careful to avoid spilling anything, which I found exceedingly tiring. I realized though that I would have to get used to my boat routine, completing certain regular jobs such as charging the batteries, seeing to the lamps, taking noon sights of the sun, and filling in the log. When I peered around the cabin everything seemed to be in good order. Fortunately I had not forgotten anything vital. All that was needed was suitable weather.

According to the law of averages we should have had a good sail, with fine and clear weather, assisted by both the NE trade winds and the Canary current, which joins the north equatorial current and then flows all the way to the West Indies. Under favourable conditions, the voyage should take just over three weeks. But I had begun on the wrong leg since I only had an east wind!

81

After breakfast I washed my dishes in seawater in order to conserve the fresh water. That entailed throwing a bucket, fastened onto a length of rope, over the side to collect it. Much care was needed in order to avoid the drag of the sea, caused by the moving boat, from snatching it out of my hands and sending the bucket down to the bottom of the sea. Then I took down the lamps from the rigging, cleaned and refilled them and stored them carefully in a cockpit seat-locker, where I also kept the paraffin. That was a messy and dirty job that I was always well pleased to have out of the way. After that I apprehensively turned the engine on. It had been coughing badly when I left my anchorage. But nothing would persuade the engine to respond. Momentarily my heart leapt into my mouth as various worrying thoughts raced through my head. I wondered whether the battery would last out until I reached land, but I finally decided that I might just have to manage without it, and comforted myself with the thought that sailing vessels in the past managed perfectly well without engines.

Since I needed to calm down, I made myself a coffee and took a cushion to lean on and jammed my feet on the opposite seat of the cockpit to savour it. Then thoughts of the last evening came to me, conjuring up the enigma of the two apparently unrelated phenomena beside each other: the sunset and the panoramic picture. It demonstrated so clearly to me how the laws of the logical and mythological consciousness were like two different languages: mythological consciousness being governed by laws stemming from the living and organic, and the other by laws governing the intellect, associated with the mechanical, dead or physical. That particular well known and profound picture of the three kings, like many others portrayed by great artists, writers and initiates, could be interpreted to be an archetypal picture of human development: the rebirth of the immortal principle in man from out of the ordinary ego or self (the true Christian rebirth).

Time had moved on and I had to take my first navigational sight of the sun on board Teassa. The only way in which I could accomplish this was by being harnessed to the wooden handrail that ran along the cockpit-roof, while seated on the cabin-roof with my feet lodged against the metal stanchions which surrounded Teassa's deck. That left my hands free to work with my sextant and write my findings on a piece of paper. I had to carefully lodge my chronometer against cushions in the cockpit where I could see it to establish the exact time of my sight. My pencil, tied on a lanyard, hung around my neck and the paper was stuck into my top pocket ready when needed. It was incredibly difficult with the lurching and heaving movements of the boat, which made me acutely conscious of the danger of being thrown overboard. I felt desperately vulnerable with no hands to hang on with. The combination of the waves and Teassa lying low in the water prevented me from having a straight horizon to bring the sun down to the mirrors of the sextant in order to measure the angle and achieve a fix. It was all very harrowing the first time and I could see that it was going to demand much patience and practice and more practice, for it was a daily task.

After I had detached myself from the harness, I took my precious instruments into the cabin and put them carefully in their boxes in the cupboard under the radio, and noted all the navigational factors that I knew in order to achieve my approximate position. This was my DR, which in navigational language means: 'The account kept of a vessel's position with regard to the course and distance made good since her position was last fixed by observations of terrestrial or celestial objects.'

I then took a turn at the tiller and tried to enjoy the afternoon. The cockpit shielded me from the chilling wind and I sought to relax in the warm sunshine and tried to still my fears. They all seemed justified under the circumstances, even though I had heard that fear remains as long as a person does not believe in God, and that ridding myself of fear would mean becoming like an island inside where refuge could be taken with the help of my guardian angel who would lead me into a safe harbour where I could rest and recover. This sounds like a pictorial allegory of a deep truth, but for me in practice – a believer in God – desperately difficult to accomplish in a small boat, alone and hurtling to possible doom. Under such circumstances the prospect of death became imminent. But, I mused, could not Death perhaps be the other face of God?

Anyway it was good to be steering myself for a while and having a direct feel of the boat in relation to the sea, which seemed to be building up in spite of the wind dropping to force two, causing a heavy helm. After three hours I thankfully handed the boat back to my first mate, for I was tired, and went into the cabin to make supper and prepare for the night so that I could turn-in early. During supper the sunset looked yellowish and ugly and was accompanied by elongated fan-shaped cirrus. I went to bed with a sense of foreboding.

I awoke around 23.00 hours. The boat had an uneasy feel to it, with sails slatting and halyards tingling against the mast. I pulled on my heavy weather clothes and went out. The wind had dwindled to force one and the heavy sea kept blocking it out, emptying the sails as we sank in the troughs. I made a hot sweet drink of Horlicks and sat down by the helm to contemplate my situation. I was still getting my sea legs, so to speak, and adjusting to the boat's ever-moving environment. The night was dark to my unaccustomed eye and I had to familiarize myself again with the melody of sounds arising from Teassa as she negotiated the sea and wind. It was rather like listening to an animated conversation: halyards slapping against spars, flowing water rippling along the hull, wind shuddering in the sails, chinking crockery and creaking wooden frames. All those sounds were accompanied by the restless sea rising and falling, breathing in great waves of harmony with the vast and living universe. I decided to hang-in for a while.

On the third day of that leg of the voyage, January 3rd at 00.30 hours, I had no alternative but to get out onto the foredeck. The wind had completely died, leaving unpleasantly high seas. I had to balance precariously, in the pitch darkness, to dowse my sails so as to counteract the formidable motion of the boat. We were well and truly becalmed.

The yacht, no longer steadied by wind, rolled and pitched abominably on the dark moody ocean, her mast and rigging wavering like a drunken sailor before the overcast sky and under the palled moon. So much for sunny consistent trade winds blowing us happily across the Atlantic! I was exhausted and very depressed. The chart indicated that we were 150 miles south of Tenerife, going nowhere, and the portents were ominous. Desperately tired, I tried to rest, but the sanguine wind dithered in making up its mind what to do next. I felt safer on watch in the cockpit. The wind languidly shifted this way and that and finally settled for the north, and by breakfast time I was able to make a westing by beating up the rising wind then at force two. That allowed me to catch up on some sleep until lunchtime when I had a vegetarian meal with a mixed salad and fruit juice. As I finished my refreshing meal I contemplated the fact that such fresh food would soon become a thing of the past. It was going to be hard. I was going to have to supplement my diet by growing some bean sprouts and cress when I settled into the long haul.

By 15.00 hours (three in the afternoon) with the wind rising, force four to five, Teassa's hull crashed into the steep waves far too heavily for comfort and we appeared to be in danger of being heaved over by waves. I was forced to choose between running and going bare-poled again. Recalling the capsize in the Biscay, I chose the former. I decided not to risk too much sail and thereby put myself in danger of swinging round at right angles to my course (broaching-to) and so facing an almost certain capsize. Rather, I chose to run under minimal sail, namely my storm sail, to help me keep a good heading and contain the speed we were coursing through the water.

My faithful first mate kept a steady course as I changed the sails, and the motion of the boat became instantly better. That was because the north wind appeared to be not so strong because its apparent speed had been reduced by the speed of the yacht. By 17.00 hours the wind swung to the north-west and steadily rose to a force six during the night.

By 07.00 hours on January 4th the strong following wind showed no signs of abating and continued building up the height of the waves. It looked as if we were heading for a full-blown gale, so I started double-checking everything in preparation for the worst, making sure all my equipment both inside and outside was secured and safely stowed away.

By noon the weather conditions prevented me from using my sextant for a sight, so I worked out my DR by other means. We had travelled approximately 194 miles south since leaving Tenerife, and the barometer was steadily rising.

During the afternoon the sun warmed the air, turning the sea blue. I no longer felt cold but the sight of the sea made me fearful. The breaking high waves were crowned with bubbling snow-white tops. I still suffered from a lack of confidence in a single hull boat with only a four-foot length keel. So I decided to sit on the coach-roof facing the bow and watch how Teassa coped. It was exhilarating in one respect and awesome in another. Teassa seemed so vulnerable. Perhaps she was over-weighted with so much storage on board and so set lower in the water than would be usual. The waves seemed colossal and Teassa so small. I sat hypnotized by the enormity of the waves and tried to estimate how far Teassa really could safely surf on the waves. That had never bothered me on 'Highwayman' with its three hulls, but it worried me in a keel-boat. The high following waves flowed down underneath the stern, lifting the hull to their crowns, and then with the sea boiling almost to the top of the rudder, we swooped down like a sea-gull into the troughs only to be picked up again by a following wave and hurled forward and up. It was alarming, but to my amazement, Teassa seemed unperturbed by it all and just took it all in her stride, sailing magnificently. I tried to attune my mind and body to these conditions, which made my adrenaline run. It was incredibly exciting although I was totally frightened. What I needed to do was to develop a sense for Teassa's abilities!

I sought the shelter of the cabin to continue my chores and eat and rest, for I had to keep body and soul together. The wind continued to harden and by 20.00 was blowing a force seven, and my fears rose with it. I tried to prepare myself for a capsize. I placed my life-jacket near me, with my calbuoy which could send out distress signals and my ditty-bag which held essentials for a period in a life raft, and I checked its contents to see if there was anything to add. The movement of the boat became so exaggerated that I had no peace on my bunk. My body continually jerked and rolled from side to side and I felt as if I was going to fall off. I decided that I would try to sleep on the floor (sole) of the cabin and packed myself in with pillows and spare clothing. I had previously slatted up the doorway, leaving one space open to allow air into the humid and stuffy cabin.

It had turned into a dreadful nightmare. Lying totally worn out and frightened out of my wits in the pitch black of the night, I listened to the screaming wind tearing at the rigging and the angry waves shaking and pressurizing the hull and hurling their weight onto the stern and throwing green water into the cockpit occasionally for good measure. I tried to imagine what might happen and prepared myself to meet it.

It had been a horrible night! The strengthening wind had increased to force eight and veered to the north-west. I hardly dared remove the slats to go out for a watch for fear of being pooped. However, at 08.00 hours – it was by then January 5th – I attached my safety harness to a ratline near the cockpit and then slatted up the door again. I could hardly equate the enormity of the sea with the smooth passage of my game little boat. The design, proportions, and lines of Teassa had in fact spoken to my soul when I first saw her on the hard near Dittisham in Devon. My sixth aesthetic sense of judgement was confirmed in the way that she ran exactly stern-on to a fast approaching wave, her bow held in line by the small sail, and how, as she accelerated down the wave, she was held by the directional stability of her deep and long straight keel before one roller after another. Logically my life appeared to be in good hands regardless of how I felt personally. I was myself the most vulnerable part of that brave little ship, and the more violent the menacing sea and wind became, the proportionally more I felt increasingly vulnerable. All that I could take credit for was that I chose the best course of action on the third day, which was to run under-canvassed.

At noon I couldn't cope with pots and pans, so ferreted under a bunk and the sole for tins of vegetarian meatloaf, potato salad, baked beans and mixed fruit salad. However I needed a tin opener. During my search I noticed that the pulverization of the hull by the sea, and the violent movement as we heaved, pitched and rolled, had dislodged some of the creaking and groaning timber structures supporting the fibre-glass skin of the hull. I also noticed that the bunk on which I had been sleeping had pulled away and was only held from collapsing by the engine casing and forward bulkhead; the structure which held the stove was also only supported by a frame fastened around the aft bulkhead leading to the bow. I wondered just how much more the boat could take.

Conditions during the evening confined me to my cabin. A gale force nine showed no signs of abating and howled and screamed incessantly, creating larger and larger waves which crashed deafeningly all around, lifting us up like a piece of flotsam and throwing us forward in a whirl of foaming water, which Teassa miraculously negotiated, calmly drawing back into the troughs like a confident sea-bird ready for the next wave. I just wished that I could share her self-assurance.

Peering through a porthole, I saw that an eerie astral twilight was exaggerating the stark condition of the fearsome and raging sea, which appeared to be in a strange state of agitation out of all proportion to anything that I had ever seen. The driving rain pierced the surface of the belligerent and menacing ocean as if with uncountable numbers of glinting swords, causing the water to rise in an array of a myriad water drops as from tiny fountains.

The violent wind, torrential rain and squalls increased in power and crescendo as the night wore on. The spectacle chilled me to my very bones but there was absolutely nothing that I could do to help myself but stay cool. I sweated profusely in the stuffy humid air of the boat and could not imagine the possibility of inflating my life raft and getting into it if necessary.

I just had to stay put and deal with my terror! My state of utter exhaustion did not help either. I felt dreamy and light-headed, as if I was being driven out of my body. Everything became an effort. It made me question if that was the spice of adventure that I had really sought for; precipitating my life into the hands of fate by placing myself alone among the vast and mighty elements of the universe, hoping thereby to discover another dimension to human life. My mind became preoccupied with recollections of the past, with events and experiences unfolding like a scroll backwards in time from that point where I had been so unceremoniously precipitated into the voyage.

Over the years, through varied interests and experiences of living on boats and developing an ever deepening love of the sea, I experienced that the water-envelope of the oceans of the earth was like a visible sphere containing within it fertile invisible forces of life which together formed a bridge by which everything spiritual crossed to enter into physical incarnation, which, in the language of the Bible, is spoken of as the Spirit of God moving on the face of the waters.

I talked with God, which I had always done quite naturally, sometimes with an appalling lack of reverence, but there were also periods where, all too human, I would fall by the wayside and lose myself in everyday consciousness. But I was always forgiven on the clear understanding that I was going to have to put all the things right that I had got wrong, however long it took, and that I had to take responsibility for myself. In other words, I held a conversation with that which I understood to be eternal, holy, divine and sacred resting behind all that ever was, is and will be.

Lying low in complete terror, exhausted, and with my heart swinging like a Yo-Yo, I begged that the storm would cease. It was totally unbearable and I felt so weak. My body lay on the cabin sole dressed for capsize and that part of myself which I call 'I' felt both inside and outside of the vulnerable body. My soul seemed expanded and part of the entire universe. I experienced the significance of the insight that we have to learn to steer the ship of our own soul. We have to become conscious of that which rests within us as part of the eternal, which is waiting to become the true helmsman of our soul. No one else could be responsible for our self but our own Self. We were truly free.

It was nearly midnight when I recalled that it was the last night of the twelve 'Holy Nights' and that next day would be Three Kings' Day. At that point all hell seemed to be let loose, with rain hammering relentlessly on the cabin roof and deck and the wind tearing at the rigging like a maddened giant, shuddering the boat angrily. I was prepared for imminent capsize. But suddenly, as if the hand of God had passed over the ocean, the wind and rain stopped momentarily. It was like a miracle. I held my breath. There was a stillness and lessening of sound. I earnestly prayed that this meant that the gale would subside. Perhaps we had been blown into the eye of the storm. Whatever the case there was a lull before it all started up again. The sea rose as high as ever, but the rage had gone out of the storm, and through the rest of the night its force dropped, and as the barometer slowly began to rise with the increasing air pressure, I gave thanks.

EIGHT   Steady Sailing then Becalmed

I sweated ever more profusely in my desperately uncomfortable life jacket in the humid and stuffy air of the sealed interior of the boat. Prepared for imminent capsize, I listened fearfully and with bated breath as the heavens opened once more, releasing cascades of blinding sleet and torrential rain to the accompaniment of the returning gale. It felt like I was in the middle of a mighty conflict between the powerful elements of the universe, as in the struggles between the mythological gods in past days. Yet, though I hardly dared to believe my ears, it appeared that the heart had gone out of the storm. The screaming and whistling through the rigging had reduced to an ear-numbing howl. The fury of the sea continued though, with the wind whipping up the ocean into a petrifying frenzy of running waves which poured into bottomless troughs and rose as high as hills above the horizon, rolling interminably in rank after rank, a vast oncoming army stretching as far as the eye could see. The danger of capsizing remained as we fled through the dark night, down the waves, before that formidable array. It only needed one rogue wave to catch up with us, and try they did. Occasionally an avalanche of green water would hurl itself into the cockpit like a giant hand reaching out to grasp hold of the stern to drag us down into the depths of the ocean. It was terrifying and awesome!

I wondered if we would ever see land again and be allowed to reach shore. It was then that I considered my family, how deeply I loved them, and recalled each one to mind. I wondered if I would ever see them again. With the prospect of death imminent, I gazed back in time and in retrospect began to see the reality of our years together, and how things had turned out. I was forced to recognize that in spite of all my hopes, ideals and dedication to motherhood, I had failed dismally.

There I was, at fifty-two, waking up from an abysmal naive stupor which had carried me unconsciously along on a tide of irrevocable circumstances. I recalled again how my father's sudden death, when I was five, literally broke my mother's heart. It left her in severe financial straits, forcing a painful change of life-style with the need to seek spiritual consolation by leaving Protestantism for Catholicism. The resultant effects of the changed social status combined with my mother's suffering from partial paralysis when I was in my teens accompanied me thereafter. Then, at the age of twenty-seven, I fell in love with a man who proved to be as equally inadequate as myself for the responsibilities demanded by a family. As with me, the reasons were initially due to circumstances beyond his control, for he was orphaned through the death of both parents by the age of five.

It all demonstrated to me that enthusiasm and naive full-hearted love and feelings of goodwill were just not enough. I had not grown up inside myself but I was still like a big undeveloped child living in an adult body. Such thoughts filled my soul with unremitting feelings of remorse and I wept in uncontrollable sorrow. I could not change the past, but wondered if I could effect some change. Eventually I must have dozed off or fallen into a state of semi-consciousness, for I experienced strange dreams and at one point became aware of a multitude of incomprehensible voices, perhaps souls, audibly penetrating through the medium of the ocean beneath the boat. Becoming agitated to an extreme intensity, they rose to an unbearable crescendo of spine-chilling sound, forcing me to cover my ears with pillows to block it all out as we coursed through the waters, the great divide lying between heaven and earth.

As the night passed, the intermittent heavy downpour of rain, which beat on the cabin roof, seemed to have a calming affect on the sea. It appeared slowly but perceptibly to flatten and push the waves down, calming the gale from a force eleven to about force eight by 08.00 hours. But since the seas remained high, it was still too dangerous to leave the cabin. I therefore stayed there, resting thankfully on the sole as Teassa courageously plunged and rose in the direction that the storm had forced us to take towards Africa, rather than our desired destination of the West

Indies. Thankfully there was still plenty of sea-room so we were in no danger of a landfall.

Although I was exhausted and traumatized by all the events, I continued my line of thought and reasoned that with the gale subsiding it looked as if I was going to be allowed to have a second chance to try to make good in the future: to turn over a new leaf, grow up and make a fresh start by facing up to the truth of how things were, and also learn to become independent. I just had to stop being dependent on my husband.

During the morning I managed to clear up the cabin and have something to eat and drink. By midday the wind was down to a steady force six, and no more green water was entering the cockpit, so I took down the top slats of the cabin door and thankfully gulped in the fresh cool air. I climbed out to the cockpit, feeling weak, and sat down. It was still awe-inspiring and I was fascinated by the spectacle of the sea and the magnificent forcefulness of the elements in their complete and absolute beauty. I was enraptured and my soul felt at one with the entire universe. The sun's warmth on my face made me feel quite dreamy, and I relaxed.

The sun's position high in the heavens signaled to me that it was noon, and that stirred in me the irrational need to know where I was, even if it was largely guess work, so that I could prepare the way for sailing again when the situation improved. I needed to orientate myself in the universe and found that working out my DR gave me extra confidence, having the effect of grounding me. After checking the log and compass, I returned to the cabin and estimated that we had been driven some eighty miles off course by the storm.

During the early evening I replaced the storm sail with my working jib and main and began to change my course. It was a relief to be sailing once more and to be able to use my bunk instead of the sole of the cabin. I remained in a weak condition though and when the wind later dropped to force five, I decided to sail with a reefed main rather than with it full, so that I would have a more restful night.

Next morning, January 7th, the north-west wind had dropped to force four and there were no more breakers. I turned back onto my old compass course of 250 degrees, with a full mainsail and my genoa. The weather, however, became unsettled by mid-afternoon, the sky clouded over and the wind dropped to force three. I therefore put up a smaller foresail. Two hours later found us in the middle of squalls and rain.

We had run out of wind by midday on January 8th. The sun came out though and I had the opportunity to dry everything that was soaked from condensation and the leaks, which had developed during our ordeal. I also aired the whole boat by opening the forward-hatch. The barometer rose steadily and occasionally a puff of wind came from the north-east, raising my spirits considerably since that was the wind that I needed. This respite also enabled me to strip and have a gloriously refreshing wash in the cockpit and attend to my smalls, which I carefully hung out to dry on the stays.

The rain came back in the late afternoon giving the impression that unsettled weather was in the offing. But after supper the barometer rose further as did the wind, which slowly built up from the NNE, and by midnight we were under full sail with a following force three wind. That called for me to put on my heavy weather clothes, and with a torch tied to a lanyard around my neck, I spent an hour and a half setting up my spinnaker-poles which allowed us to sail goose-winged and to take full advantage of the light wind throughout the night.

The wind and sea built up through the day of January 9th and even though we were on an uncomfortable course, we were on our way, heading in a south-westerly direction, sailing down the latitudes. I realized that the unsettled weather which I had been experiencing was due to the fact that I was in an area called the Variables, a band stretching east to west above the Trades, and that it was likely that the gale and the north-east wind had extended this region further down. The wind charts indicated that latitude 15 degrees was best for the trade wind, so that was where we were heading. By evening time we had a running sea and force five to six wind, and yawed to starboard continually and surfed too rapidly for my peace of mind, for I still needed to assess whether I was courting danger unnecessarily. Waves often humped up against the stern, precipitating us forward in an alarming fashion, causing the boat to yaw off course. I still suffered from the inexperience of such conditions in a keel boat, but I had to get the balance right.

The night was clear and moonlit, apart from a few scattered white clouds, and the heavens were studded with brilliant stars, affording good visibility. I had decided to lessen my sail area to facilitate a more comfortable passage, because I was exhausted and needed to rest.

During an early watch on the morning of January 10th, I still felt that the boat was out of control but I left things as they were. Later in the day I was delighted to pick up the beacon from the Cape Verde Islands, the last archipelago off the West Coast of Africa. It verified my position, confirming my DR and the sight that I had taken at noon. That cheered me no end, giving me confidence that I would find my way across the Atlantic. We had covered our first 605 miles.

The wind dropped and veered northwards during the night, but on the morning of January 11th I felt very strange, so let the boat sail itself during the rest of the day while I lay in my bunk. My legs felt wobbly and my heart pounded alarmingly if I exerted myself. I wondered if I was going to have a heart attack. I knew that I was totally exhausted and that the situation was probably due to lack of sleep and food (for I had lost my appetite), or not drinking enough so causing dehydration since I had been conserving water. Apart from those problems, my body was also full of aches and pains. I had been thrown about unmercifully, and banged against obstacles in an effort to retain my balance, and had swung from the rigging like a trapeze artist when putting up sails. I had bruises on my head from hitting the chart table and bunk when thrown backwards while making my bed, and I had a hugely swollen right knee from skidding uncountable times against deck-fittings when the boat rolled and yawed. I also had incredibly sore hands, which throbbed relentlessly. Slumped on my bunk like an old bag of sails, I felt very sorry for myself. Even getting myself a drink seemed too much effort. When I talked to myself to try to pull myself together, my voice sounded as if it came from far away.

The next day, January 12th at eight in the morning, there was a north-westerly force four wind blowing and I persuaded myself to have some breakfast in the cockpit. I was so glad not to be facing another sail change, so could continue to nurse my energies. The day became bright and sunny, making me feel that I had nothing to worry about, but I found the sea and elements too energetic and intimidating, so went back into the cabin. I cleared away my breakfast things and decided that I would try to read a book by perching on my bunk and placing bags of clothes between my back and the hull and bracing my legs against my lifejacket, all supported by the lee-board. But anxieties persisted in soaring around in my mind, like a flock of seagulls, causing a kind of paralysis. I wondered why I was taking such a long time over my Atlantic crossing compared with others, and whether my battery would go flat and my food and water run out, and whether I would regain my strength and manage to enter port without an engine. But I had to put a stop to these whirling thoughts. I realized that this could be done by doing

94

something practical, so I began to check my sack of potatoes in the bow, removing shoots and bad potatoes even though I was unwell, for it diverted my mind from those hopeless circling thoughts.

The temperature cooled by late afternoon, so I prepared everything ready for the night and then went out and sat on the cabin roof. I faced the bow, watching it rise and fall as it sliced through the blue sea, which streamed past the hull, leaving a bubbly, silver wake.

Later the evening wind chilled me as it blew coldly on my back, but it felt as if it was losing its strength. Then the beautiful setting sun warmed my face and the clouds in the blue heavens flew like great white birds with necks outstretched, winging their way to the north pursued by all kinds of fascinating forms like determined heroes riding fiery winged horses rearing in protest but galloping in pursuit. I felt reassured and told myself that I had no need to worry. We were making a good passage, and I knew my position. Teassa was also fine and I would pick up my strength. I determined then to see every new day as one nearer home!

By January 13th we had covered nearly 900 miles. This meant that we were approaching the half-way mark. However we had almost run out of wind yet again and I had to dismiss negative thoughts because otherwise I would have fallen into despair. The thought of Eve, whom I had deserted, could reduce me to floods of tears only too easily. It was also depressing to face up to the realization that though I was approaching the middle of my crossing, I really had not enjoyed the sail. I just had to keep my mind on a middle road and not let my thoughts wander about like a crazy barometer. I consoled myself with the thought that I was still not my old self because of my wobbly legs and fluttering heart.

Later that day, I realized that the log numbers were not spinning properly and so I had to dismantle the log and examine it to see what was wrong. The works had seized up due to constant exposure to seawater and needed cleaning and oiling. The propeller had barnacles on it, which needed to be scraped off, and the line was fraying and had weed attached to it and it desperately needed replacing. All this took the best part of the morning and left no time for anything like worrying thoughts or boredom setting in. Boredom was not a problem though, for there was always something to do on board a boat, and anyway I had schooled myself to use my time constructively, such as to read challenging books and as a consequence have things to think about.

Well the wind dropped again and the motion of the boat became easier. I was therefore able to rest and sleep reasonably comfortably for a long stretch of twelve hours. When I awoke in the morning, I felt a great deal better and more at peace with myself.

On the morning of January 14th we found ourselves becalmed. The log was close to the 1,000 mile mark on the chart, and we had been at sea for two weeks. I celebrated this fact by having my favourite breakfast even though we were becalmed. I had chips and two slices of bacon from the joint, and fried them along with an egg. It was delicious! Then I sat in the cockpit, sipped a mug of coffee and took stock of my situation.

Being becalmed enabled me to inspect my equipment, stores and running gear in preparation for the next thousand or so miles and also to clean, wash and dry my clothes and generally tidy up and air the boat. I started with myself, and had a refreshing wash before putting on clean clothes. Feeling more comfortable, I finished the washing and hung it up to dry in the sun, and then carefully fastened my damp sleeping bag over the boom so that it would not slip off. Then I opened the forward hatch so that the air could pass through the boat and dry up the condensation. Water that dribbled down the hull, for instance, had found its way onto my precious charts lying under the bunk mattress beneath the chart table. I had to dry and repair them and then roll them up and put them in a plastic bag. I then wiped down all the hull surfaces within reach, which were by then showing signs of black mould. I was decidedly tired after all these exertions so had a break.

After lunch I still needed to rest for I needed to conserve my strength. During the rest of that day I noted down all items in need of repair or replacement and then cleared up and fell into my bed.

We were still becalmed the next day, January 15th. The sea had died down and the sun shone from a clear blue sky, so I continued to examine and repair equipment such as the cord on my Hassler steering gear which needed replacing and my old white genoa sail needed to be patched and another sail repaired.

At noon there was the straightest horizon that anyone could possibly wish for. It was perfect for a sight and fix. I never ceased to wonder at how satisfying it was to achieve that with the aid of my beautiful instruments: the sextant and chronometer. It was quite magical!

Not many people know that the ability to determine one's longitude is a comparatively recent accomplishment. Mariners used to sail along known latitudes but have no idea when they were going to meet land. Back in AD 150, the cartographer and astronomer, Ptolemy, chose the Equator as the zero degree parallel of latitude because that was where the sun passed almost directly overhead. Likewise the Tropic of Cancer and the Tropic of Capricorn, two other famous parallels, assumed their positions due to the sun. The two tropics marked the northern and southern boundaries of the sun's apparent motion over the course of the year. In Ptolemy's time it was understood that anyone living below the equator would melt due to the terrible heat. For his prime meridian, the zero degree of longitude, Ptolemy chose a line from north to south passing through the Canary Islands, originally known as the Fortunate Islands. It was a political choice rather than one derived from nature. Discovering one's latitude was relatively easy but finding one's longitude was virtually impossible because it depended on very accurate time measurements. The exact time on board had to be compared with that at the home-port or other place of known longitude, and there were no clocks accurate enough for this purpose until the second half of the eighteenth century. Then an English genius, a clockmaker, created a mechanism whose accurate time keeping made the calculation of longitude possible. Today we take it for granted that each hour's difference between the vessel and the starting point marks a progress of fifteen degrees of longitude, but this is comparatively recent knowledge.

In the Age of Discovery, during the late fifteenth and early sixteenth century, every great sea captain became lost at sea, even Francis Drake. It was thought then that sailors arrived at their destination as a result of good luck and the grace of God. For example, in a single accident on 22nd October 1707 near the Scilly Isles, four homeward bound British warships ran aground, nearly losing two thousand men. They simply did not know where they were. Well at least I did know where I was, and I took heart from such knowledge. It seemed so unbelievable to me that once upon a time the vital compass and useful clock were regarded as instruments of black magic practices.

I gazed balefully at the variable and uncertain weather. The wind was flukey and accompanied by scattered cloud mixed with bright sunshine and occasionally light intermittent showery rain. Then, to my amazement, a radiant rainbow emerged in the sky ahead. It was breathtaking and immensely exciting. I wondered if it could be a good omen similar to the one after the great flood recorded in the Bible when God said 'I do set this bow in the cloud, and it shall be a token of a covenant between me and the earth.'

Well the presence of this exquisite phenomenon was a boost to my spirit because for me it was the visible manifestation of the otherwise invisible World Soul. It was a manifestation of the Eternal Feminine: a primordial Woman, the very womb of the creation arrayed in the colours arising from the deeds and sufferings of light in its cosmic conflict with realms of darkness. I felt confident that I was beholding the living form of the Soul of the Universe, which connected the world of the spirit to the world of the senses. The ancient Egyptians had called this feminine power in the universe by the name of Isis. The individual who was able to lift her veil, to perceive her, was held to have completed their inner voyage and seen their own Higher Self. Indeed the Greeks believed that the secret of human existence lay in the fact that every individual person bore within them a copy of the Soul of the Universe. It was my task, through my voyage, to find the way for my soul to bridge those two worlds: that of the senses and the spirit, and like the Vikings, find the Gjallard Bridge where humans could converse with the gods. All too soon though, the rainbow vanished as if it had never been, and I fell back to earthly reality.

The wind had slowly picked up during the night, blowing in a north-westerly direction at around force two or three. By midnight the wind had increased to force four and beat comfortably under our main sail and genoa. This helped to facilitate a better night's sleep. But during the very early hours of January 16th, the wind decreased once more.

Next day the barometer and the wind dropped slowly throughout the morning and the boat struggled to keep sailing in the light wind, with the sails slatting and banging miserably when we were left without wind. It felt as if we were in the doldrums and I feared that the voyage was likely to become the longest on record. At that point I felt a kinship with Coleridge's Ancient Mariner:

> 'Down dropt the breeze, the sails dropt down
> 'Twas sad as sad could be;
> And we did speak only to break
> The silence of the sea!'

It was so diabolically frustrating to sit helplessly on a mirror-like sea, especially in my circumstances, but as there was absolutely nothing I could do about it, I sought refuge in my bunk.

NINE   Halfway Point, seeking the Trade Winds

There was still no wind by the morning of January 18th, so I sat on the foredeck with a strong coffee and stared gloomily at my windless, watery wilderness. Once more I wondered dolefully what I was really seeking with my lone voyage.

After further thought, I tentatively concluded that I was searching for an ultimate psychic energy, which like love itself, was not to be attained second hand, but could conceivably be by individual effort. Perhaps this explained why myself and others like me, in seeking for such integration, sought to go alone into vast and lonely places in order to free our individual mind from the overwhelmingly powerful collective mind of society.

I felt cold and hungry once more and so made my way to the galley with the thought that an early lunch might cheer me up. I made a meal of stewed steak, mashed potatoes and peas, after which I took a book to the cockpit with a view to resting there. I was in fact still recovering from the storm and had to recognize that my energy was limited. But on leaving the cabin I noticed that the barometer was creeping up. That gave grounds for hope, and so I settled down comfortably on my makeshift couch and relaxed, giving myself up to the rolling, rocking motion of the boat.

While dreamily watching the sea in a semi-hypnotic state, with the sun shining brilliantly from its zenith, I had a strange experience. The entire surface of the ocean began to become peculiarly agitated, and countless sparkling pyramid-like shapes emerged and rose as if the waters of the ocean were seeking to become air-borne. It seemed as though the starry sky was mirrored in the sea by countless eyes looking up to the heavens from within the forms. On the one hand I had a sense of fear in my soul and on the other, I wondered if my imagination was running riot. Yet it was extraordinary and eerily beautiful in its own fashion. The phenomena did not last for long though and I sensed that it was possibly indicating a change in the sea and weather conditions.

During the afternoon I grilled two slices of cheese-on-toast, made a mug of tea, and sat on the fore deck with my back propped up against the cabin windows. I faced the bow and wished to enjoy the open view of the Atlantic and contemplate the strange sea phenomena of the morning. I thought about imagination which was such an illusive experience and hard to define. Modern education, it seemed to me, based the natural sciences on only two realms of experience: reason and sense perception. Imagination was totally ignored and nature, with its images portrayed through art and religious conviction, was considered as less real than things in themselves. Lamentably, imagination was forced to recede into the background of the mind and become a neglected faculty. But for me it was a matter of seeing more than I could tell and understanding more than I could see.

My attempts to study spiritual life from a scientific point of view sometimes approached the experience of being able to see inwardly and intuitively, in a sacred way, with my mind's eye, the form of things within their dimension of spirit and in their relationship of the part to the whole. However, sometimes I thought that I had grasped something profound only for it to vanish as in a dream, and I had to work once more to build up an understanding on which to build further comprehension. I had become convinced however that imagination was the central faculty of the soul, acting as a bridge between the senses and the intellect (the body and mind) and spirit and matter.

I felt chilled to the bone and so stood up, gathered together my things, and returned my mug and plate to the galley. I then pulled on a sea-jersey and decided to have a general check around the deck well before it became dark. Without wind, the mighty ocean was silent, its swell smooth, with no wrinkles to be seen except when Teassa rolled languidly like a whale wallowing lazily in the sunshine, creating ripples of disturbance.

There was still no wind during the evening, but my night watch in Teassa's cockpit on the dark silky sea was gladdened by the glorious sight of countless stars shining in the sky of the heavenly universe. Some were in the far distance and others close, with some moving in orbits and others settled in constellations. They seemed to be speaking a secret language of their own, moving in communion with the vibrant, living earth cradled in their midst as she inhaled deeply within herself, bringing the old year and winter to its end. Yet in continuing that mighty rhythm, she would release her breath, giving rise to the new year and its seasons, in one glorious exhalation reaching into the vast expanses of the universe and bringing the resurrection of life to all her kingdoms – visibly expressed in the burgeoning of flowers and newborn creatures in Spring.

The time passed slowly without a breath of air in the calm night. All sails had been sheeted back and halyards belayed to prevent them slapping endlessly in an irritating way against the mast. I was comfortably warm and fully awake but remained in the cockpit for I couldn't sleep. I needed to still the fears arising in my mind and oppressing my soul as a result of being becalmed. I had to discipline my thoughts and quell all feelings of anxiety because it was going to be a long night for me.

Right from the beginning of the voyage I had on various occasions attempted to look back at areas of my varied and complicated life in order to make some sense of it, and I continually came up against the problem of memory. My faculty of memory seemed so poor, sporadic and unreliable. It dwindled away over time, leaving me to recall little or nothing before the age of five. It appeared to me that human memory had become a kind of veil over the unconscious processes of the soul and that we only had a fragmentary experience of time because we never experienced it in its completeness. It appeared that the stream of time emerged continually from an unknown nothingness, and the darkness from which it sprang we called the future and the darkness into which it vanished we called the past. What we knew of the fleeting moment of the present was born out of an unconscious experience that time flowed through us. Even for the very abstract intellect of the modern age, the future gleamed dimly as probability and possibility, while the dull light of remembrance threw fading colours of memory over the quickly receding past before it finally disappeared into forgetfulness. Those who were satisfied with 'a measly trickle of consciousness', enough to continue a day-to-day existence, could easily reconcile themselves to living permanently between these two realms of darkness. But to someone like myself, embarking on an 'inner voyage', it became vital to transcend the boundary set by memory in order to overcome the darkness of forgetting, and to transform the vague foreboding of the future into a certainty of vision, and in such a manner to reach beyond the fleeting glory of the moment to the true experience of the present, to experience the eternal in the now, the God-in-us.

The important question for me was to discover just how far the human memory could reach back, and that if it could reach back to the moment when personal memory began then what type of consciousness was there beyond that. I wondered if consciousness was synonymous with memory, for I could see that it was memory which bonded together a sequence of experiences as the unique possession of an individual who called themselves by that name common to all and yet unique to each person: 'I'.

What a moment of deepest significance it was when, in learning to speak, a child first called itself by the word 'I'. Every other word could be learnt by imitation, but that single word could only be spoken out of the realization of self-consciousness. That moment of self-conscious ego being, or I-AM-ness, was for me the barrier, the 'Great Divide' through which I longed to penetrate. Most people could remember backwards to their fourth year, but very few could ever recall that magic moment in which they first said 'I'. I certainly could not! For me the life of a growing child reflected within itself something of the history of all mankind and that significant moment of self-consciousness corresponded to what was known in biblical symbolism as 'the Fall of Man from Paradise'.

I believe that someone like the little-known seventeenth century poet, Thomas Traherne, had passed that barrier and that some things that he wrote were pertinent to my problem. He had said, with such infant memories in mind: 'Our Saviour's meaning when He said, ye must be born again and become as little children that will enter the Kingdom of Heaven, is far deeper than is generally believed.'

Similarly Ralph Waldo Emerson has said, 'Infancy is the perpetual Messiah, which comes to the arms of fallen men and pleads with them to return to paradise.' This situation was also obviously a reality for Wordsworth when he wrote his 'Ode on Intimations from Recollections of Childhood', where he pointed to the pre-natal origins of the soul and the human capacity for experiencing, at certain moments, that frontier which the soul crossed at birth.

I really wished to find a way to pass that 'Great Divide'! Indeed what I wanted to know through experience with all my heart was whether that essentially personal element, the human 'I' or ego, was in fact a spiritual entity, having its origins in a spiritual world from which it had come to birth in a physical body. I sought to find hidden faculties in my soul to help reveal how all the kingdoms of nature were fashioned, informed and sustained by invisible forces originating from a spiritual cosmos. I still anticipated that the loneliness, danger, terror, privation and hardship of a single-handed ocean voyage, might, like the trials of initiation in ancient times, act as a kind of catalyst and precipitate me towards a spiritual awakening and towards a transcendent enlightenment.

I was beginning to see how my living through the daily experiences of the first fifty two years of my life, had been unconsciously and consciously a struggle on an inward path in preparation for my outer voyage, so that I would have some idea of what to expect in the geography of inner space if such an awakening should take place. So at least I had discovered an answer to the question posed by as to why I had chosen to sail alone in a small boat. I gained clarification that my undertaking of a lone voyage is certainly not the whim of a moment but rather the result of a lifetime of earnest striving towards a spiritual goal.

On the morning of January 19th, a slightly rising breeze from the NNW enabled me to use my genoa sail and to ghost along aided by the ocean current. I celebrated by cooking my favourite breakfast and anticipated that with the more pleasant motion of the boat, I would be able to catch up on sleep. I actually thought that I had benefited from the enforced rest caused by being becalmed. It had enabled me to nurse a painful bruised elbow and swollen right knee and to stay off my unsteady legs. Unfortunately though, because I had been sitting whenever I could in order to conserve my energy, I had developed an aching bottom. But in spite of this I felt better, and it was a fine day.

After taking my noon sight, I established that I had reached Latitude 15 degrees and Longitude 33, so I expected to experience the trade winds at that point. Because I was not technically or mathematically inclined, I found the ability to confirm my position through tables and observations to within a pinpoint on a chart, absolutely magical.

By mid-afternoon the wind slowly dropped but an occasional puff of wind in the small foresail helped us keep a heading into the evening gloom, which enfolded us within shrouds of inky-black darkness. This however was slowly drawn aside by an indescribably beautiful moon rising above the darker edge of the moody sea: a silver sliver of gleaming light accompanied by a brilliant star, both set like sparkling gems against a band of crystal clear blue-green sky expanding into the heavens, themselves studded with brilliant stars that shone intermittently between the clouds. The sight stimulated me to become inwardly aware in my heart of the wonders of creation, which I had not grasped with my thinking. As in a dream, I became enveloped in the mighty symphony of sound and movement within the vast universe and was imbued with an intense sense of wonder, for I suddenly realized that the stars were not rising, as I had always understood. Rather it was a case of my being gently, silently and perceptibly carried eastwards by the revolving earth and turning into the stars in the opposite direction to the one in which I was sailing in my boat with the variable aid of the wind and ocean currents. The current actually flowed westwards in the opposite direction to the earth's spin. It was a deep encompassing revelation for me – an inner grasping rather than an intellectual one – marking an important turning point in my comprehension of our earthly reality.

On January 20th there was no wind at all and it was very hard not to be depressed by this combined with the fact that it was Eve's birthday. I longed to be at home with her and I could not remember ever having missed her birthday before. She would be twelve.

In a heavy mood, I prepared my breakfast of cereal, a boiled egg and toast and wondered what I could do to celebrate this special day. Finally I decided to light a candle before each meal during the day, read a birthday verse, and send her my love and think about her life. I sat on the edge of my bunk, watching the small burning flame of the candle. This drew my thoughts together, and made me recollect the end of the year 1967.

The whole family had sailed by stages in our boat, called Highwayman, to Dartmouth in Devon from Castropol in northern Spain, where we had been living for almost a year. Christmas was approaching so we arranged to stay in the warm and welcoming Boatel, situated across the river from where our boat was moored, at least until the baby that I was carrying was born. The birth of Eve occurred early in the morning of January 20th and was a moment in time that I shall never forget, for as that tiny baby entered into the world, and I received her into my arms, I felt encompassed by a warm, profound, and light-filled subliminal sense of love. That was an experience I hoped to carry within my soul throughout eternity. I called her 'Eve Maria'.

After blowing out the candle and clearing up my breakfast things, I sat and watched the smooth, gently rolling surface of the sea mirroring the colour of the sky with its waters intermingling subtly with the air and light, and with its depths teaming with life. I thought how the human soul was so much like the water which came from heaven and rising, returned there: ever returning and eternally changing throughout evolution. I recalled how Heraclitus, the Greek philosopher and teacher at the Temple of Ephesus, had described the human soul saying, 'You will never be able to fathom her boundaries, even when you tread all existing roads, so extensive is her being'. When I recalled this, it raised more questions within me – I wondered if those wise thoughts helped to explain the experience of my own emptiness when alone, and whether they could help me to face-up to myself by looking within. I further wondered whether the emptiness of the apparent void, the space between that of the universe and earth, was a mirror of humanity's condition, and that we could not comprehend the being of the soul in our modern age because it could not be seen with the physical eye.

I then remembered how during the storm, the fear of imminent death seemed to trigger the need for my soul to draw into sharp focus the details and events of my life. And then while I lay at rest on my bunk during the morning, I moved in memory from the present back in time in the manner of an expanding fan. What I beheld was a bewildering panorama: a family in constant movement over a period of twenty-five years from its conception, and then my own eight years in community: five in the Camphill Village Community, three in the Auxiliary Territorial Service, and then eighteen years spent at school and living at home. I just had no idea what the purpose of it all was and where it was supposed to lead. One thing that I was certain of though was that only Eve needed me. The rest of the family had drawn away to pursue their own paths of destiny. I had to confront the chastening experience that I had been hanging on blindly to something that was no longer a reality: the sense of belonging to a family that needed me, a family where there had been so much shared love and which had been the centre and joy of my life. In itself, love enabled me to carry the family through an endless chain of torturous circumstances, initially caused by Trevor's inability to remain in any one occupation for any length of time and therefore provide a secure and permanent home life. Then with his decision to become a writer at the age of forty-nine, we were finally reduced to a state of abject poverty which destroyed our accustomed style of life and all the hopes and dreams that I harboured for my children.

I found these thoughts very dispiriting and so began to tackle practical jobs to distract my mind from further negativity. I thoroughly checked

106

my supplies and came to the conclusion that I had enough for at least another three weeks. This buoyed up my confidence considerably. Nevertheless, as a precaution, I decided to cut down on my intake. Though initially I had no idea that my voyage would take so long, I had fortunately prepared for this eventuality.

I accepted the enforced rest and the lack of wind as a blessing in disguise. My body was recovering and I was beginning to feel more at peace with myself, and even resigned to not making it across the Atlantic. I did not feel quite my old self but was regaining my appetite and I no longer needed to force myself to eat. I found though that I could not tolerate food being cooked in salt water, so I had to keep a tight control on my thirst in order to conserve fresh water. Unfortunately I had had no success in growing bean shoots as a source of fresh food!

During the afternoon a welcome NNE wind arose and by late evening we were well under sail. At midnight the wind continued NNE and rose to force four. Teassa's white, enlivened wake streamed vigorously astern, raising my hopes high and allowing me to climb thankfully into my sleeping bag.

On the morning of January 21st the wind was NNE between force four and five and the barometer was well up. However, sailing was difficult and tiring. Teassa writhed and heeled as I forced a course across short high waves and the south-westerly current in order to make a westing across the Atlantic. I exhausted myself trying out various sail combinations throughout the day without success. Even reducing sail and speed did not help. The wind chart indicated extra strong winds in the area.

At one point, when I was working with the sails, I saw something zip past high in the air above my bow and I thought it was a bird. But on reflection I decided that we were too far from land and anyway it did not look like a bird. Then I saw it once more and realized it was a flying fish. I didn't know they could fly so high, and up and down like a bird. It was so amazing, soaring right up into the sky as if trying to reach the very heavens themselves, shimmering and sparkling in the sun, and then skimming back into the water with a loud plop.

As the day passed the wind dropped, and towards late evening it died completely. It was unbelievable.

The arrival of January 22nd made me realize that three weeks had passed since we left Tenerife. There was only an occasional light breeze, but with the help of the current and ghosting we had arrived at the halfway mark on my chart, which raised my spirits considerably. Seeking for the trade winds, I dropped slightly below latitude 15, and continued in a westerly direction. Basically, what I had to do was to steer slightly more to port or starboard off the general direction, according to whether my sights indicated that we were too far to north or south.

Feeling more comfortable about the voyage, I cleaned the stove and its surrounding area and the ceiling, which was black with soot from my paraffin-light that I used at night. Then, after lunch, I inspected my clothes, stored in plastic bags, to make sure that they were not going mouldy. Then I heard what I thought was a loose sheet flapping about in the cockpit, so I put down my sewing and climbed out to see. It was a flying fish that had been trying to escape, lying on its back with wings outspread and gasping its last. I hesitated to throw it back, for I longed for fresh food, but it was too late, for it stopped breathing.

Its beauty was truly astonishing. Its back was patterned with pretty red-brown scales, underlain with the most beautiful pale purple tinged with sky blue. Its underside was silvery and its large dark eyes spoke to my heart. Its wings were like gossamer, tinctured with delicate hues of brown and fringed in transparent blue. It was no wonder that those fish, when shooting up from under the bow, looked like fairy fish. They sparkled in the sun as they sped through the air, having launched themselves from the back of a wave with a stroke of their tails, soaring some forty-five feet in the air. It was with misgiving that I thankfully prepared my sacrificial gift from the sea. It was delicious!

There was still no wind on January 23rd. I felt hopeless and helpless and sat on my bunk listening to the water moving along the hull, feeling the roll of the boat and hearing the slap of the halyards against the mast. I had absolutely no sense of being in the middle of the watery wilderness of the Atlantic. Here was a real lesson in patience and trust.

Again looking for an occupation, I took the opportunity to clean out the bilges. This is a horrible, smelly job for the bilges collect dirt and everything that spills or seeps in from other parts of the boat: seawater, oil, paraffin, and spillage during cooking. The sides and frames proved to be slimy and difficult to clean with seawater.

In the afternoon I sat in the cockpit and repaired clothes that were showing signs of wear and tear, and I again thought about my voyage. I had really enjoyed the experience of being able to move about freely in what I would call exclusively a man's world: the world of boats, voyages and adventure. I loved to share their comradely and noncommittal friendship, the mutual interest in and love of the sea with its dangers, and also the sense of caring and concern, and willingness to offer a hand, which I had never found on shore. Thinking about this, I was interested to realize that this was not a quality that I shared with Trevor. I realized that as a wife in the first place, and a woman in the second, I was not considered an equal, and when circumstances altered from a period of dependence on my support to one where it was not needed, I was rejected and expected to maintain myself, invariably with children, until my assistance was wanted again. I had to acknowledge how I had always admired that other outgoing, adventurous, pioneering world of men, and how I lamented the limitations of my particular state of perpetually oppressed and limited womanhood. I slowly began to realize that my subjugation was due to conditioning, ignorance, immaturity, naiveté, and especially an undeveloped thought life, pointing to a lack of consciousness.

Thankfully, a rising NNW wind greeted January 24th, so we ghosted through the morning. By midday, when I had completed my DR position, the wind changed to a north-easterly between force two and three. We appeared to be finally picking up the trade winds. However, I waited before changing sails, to make certain that the wind stayed constant. In the light of that decision, lunch seemed a good idea.

After eating, my heart filled with hope and I joyfully set up my spinnaker poles. It took about an hour and a half sorting them out with all the fittings to the halyards, sails, and sheets. Though I was glad to be on the move once more, I had to fight the sea, which continued to pull the boat too far south on my westward compass course. This made me realize that a bigger boat with a powerful engine would have been more suitable under such circumstances, and that Teassa was too small.

During the evening, while I was sitting reading on my bunk, there was a terrific thump on the hull. At first I thought that something had broken and so I rushed out of the cabin and into the cockpit to look. There was nothing to be seen anywhere to indicate what it was. I therefore assumed that it must have been a large marine mammal in collision with the hull of the boat.

The next day, January 25th, started disappointingly with an inconsistent wind throughout the morning, finally moving from NNE and settling to NE by afternoon. The sky, dark with clouds, reflected my own mood. Judging by the progress made during the past two days, I reasoned that it would take a further four to five weeks to cross the Atlantic. I therefore decided to cut down further on the use of my supplies, particularly water, and strictly ration my favourite foods like salted bacon that made my mouth water, and apples and oranges, which were so refreshing. However, even though I felt sorry for myself, I was basically fit and well and could cope with rationing.

When resting, I liked to read material about the spiritual dimension to life from a scientific point of view. I hoped that it would help me prise open a chink to allow me to look into the spiritual world in contrast to the material world where everything could be seen and handled and so be proven to exist. The spiritual world, for me, can be sensed intuitively as lying deep within my soul, a world whose warp and weft lies hidden within the fabric of the experience of material life. Yet I could not penetrate, unveil, or prove that it existed in the usual sense of the word. I longed to tangibly experience the interrelationship between the earth and the universe and my place and task as a part of humanity in the great drama. I was however beginning to understand how the being of the soul was the 'key to the universe'. For me the Greek word 'psychology' actually meant 'knowledge of the soul', while the modern interpretation of the word was: 'an understanding of human nature'. Unfortunately that definition rejected the existence of the soul and as such was characteristic of everyday materialistic thinking.

In the middle of the night I had a peculiar experience. I was woken from sleep by a voice urgently calling my name – "Shirley". I shot out of my bunk and into the cockpit, but there was no one there. I looked all around but there was absolutely nobody to be seen. I felt shattered!

TEN   Borne on the Trades to Barbados

On the morning of January 26th the wind had settled, so I dared to think that it was the long sought after trade wind. If that was so, then I did not have to worry about a change of course and sails. I decided therefore to celebrate by catching a fish to supplement my diet of mainly dried and tinned foods. I unwound the line from its wooden frame, fastened on my spinner, and allowed it to trail into the sea astern. I then played half-heartedly on the line, for I was not very familiar with the skills of fishing, and eventually gave up with no success. I therefore secured the frame to a deck cleat and left the line trawling in the sea so that I could get on with other tasks needing my attention.

I prepared a complicated meal of curried beef, peas and rice, but suffered the usual mishap of spillage and wandering utensils due to the erratic heaving motion of the boat, and half of the meal was burnt by being too economical with water. It made such a ghastly stink! But I ate what I could and then cleared up. Then I remembered that I had a line out, and went into the cockpit to pull it in. It felt heavy, but I was not convinced that I had caught anything. However it was evident that I had because of the vigorous tugging on the end of the line, which excited me.

With extreme care I drew the line in. The fish came nearer and must have been a foot long. I could see a kind of sulphuric-green flashing in the water and then a strange shaped head appeared with a black knobby-spine leading to a shark-like tail. I did not like the look of it at all! Hauling it gingerly on board I gave it a wide birth as it slithered over the side and flopped onto the floor of the cockpit and flapped frantically, trying to return to the sea. The spine was in fact a gorgeous blue from which markings in blue curved down round the green of its elongated, boney body. I assumed that it would not be good to eat and, with relief, gingerly released it from the hook and threw it back to sea. On the one hand, I was not hungry enough at that time to eat such an uninviting fish, and on the other, my feelings were confused about the whole matter of hunting and killing in order to eat.

At midday the sun burst through the clouds and I was able to take a noon sight and identify my position. It was a beautiful sunny day. My spinnaker poles and genoas spread out gracefully like the wings of a bird in welcome embrace of the NE wind for yet another day. The long sought after NE trade winds gained in strength, and as the barometer rose my spirits rose with it.

My reckoning was that I had 1,200 miles to sail before reaching the West Indies. It felt simply marvellous to have the wind blowing constantly from the right direction, and I was encouraged to trail my neglected and unfamiliar fishing line and spinner astern again. To my extreme surprise there was an almost immediate pull on the line and I caught my second fish, but it was too small to eat and since I was not entirely happy about eating it, I threw it back into the sea. Another try eventually produced an edible-looking fish, which I reluctantly killed and ate thankfully for supper.

Fishing reminded me of Tristan, my third child, when aged fifteen, excitedly catching large Blues from the side of the dock where we were living on 'Tahanni' our 49 foot Trident Trimaran then moored off City Island, New York. Sadly, I recalled how that once we were so close to one another as mother and son, almost inseparable in fact. He had all the noble, warm-hearted qualities of a young knight, but life moved on relentlessly. It was the combination of ever-changing circumstances, adolescence, and Trevor's new interest in him as a young adult rather than as a child, particularly that over-riding influence as father and man-of-the-world, which changed our relationship irrevocably.

The trade winds continued to blow at force four to five throughout the day of January 27th. The spinnaker poles remained set with genoas, accompanied by the main sail, which I had secured by a guy rope to steady the boom and prevent the sail chaffing against the stays. The guy and sheets had to be checked and trimmed on a regular basis to get the best out of the boat. That is to say, the sails had to be tightened or loosened with the help of the winches in the cockpit. Aided by these adjustments, we made rapid progress.

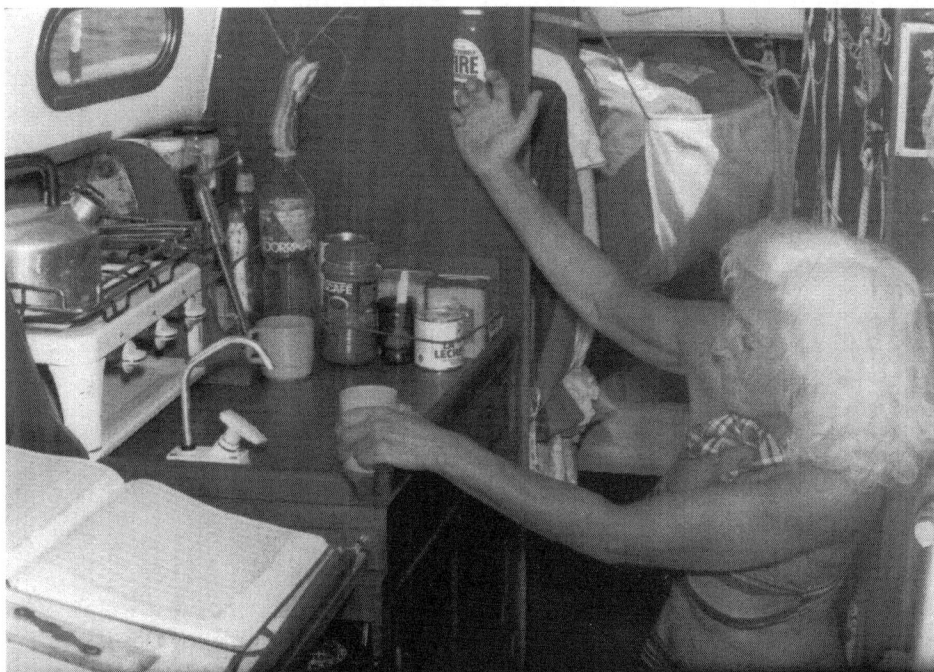

Manoeuvring in Teassa's Kitchen

After breakfast I adjusted my self-steering gear and noticed that we were accompanied by ten or so small, brown fishy companions. Their undersides were blue and they appeared to like swimming behind the rudder. Perhaps Teassa's slipstream was restful for them and the vegetation attached to her deep hull seemed enticing to eat.

I also observed a bird which I had seen flying high above the mast during the previous two weeks, which I had assumed to be one of several. Yet we were at that point just too far from land for this to be the case, so it appeared that the bird was crossing the Atlantic with me. Dear God, what a beautiful gift: a winged messenger through whom my angel could intimate that I was not really alone. New confidence filled my heart and soul, and without inhibition I cried out aloud with joy and happiness, improvising a song of greeting and thankfulness to my accompanying friend who sailed in effortless circles in the heavens above me.

The sea and sky were imbued with varied nuances of blue, relieved by froth-crested waves and scattered white clouds. The constant warmth of the sun invited me to spend the day with no clothes on, with the exception of when I needed to sit on the hot slats of the cockpit seats or the fibre-glass roof or deck. Then I needed to put on my bikini bottom and sit on a towel for protection. When the sun became excessively hot towards midday, I pulled out the orange PVC tarpaulin from the bow and secured it over the cabin roof to keep the inside of the cabin cool. After taking my morning sight, I escaped from the blazing sunshine into the cool interior of the cabin to plot my position and cook my lunch and have a rest.

In the afternoon I checked my log line to see that it was free from slippery, slimy plant life, which liked to grow on it, and then I relaxed by lying on the towel-covered floorboards supported by the cockpit seats. Wearing a fisherman's straw hat for protection, I propped up my head with a cushion and lost myself in the book that interested me at that time. Then something made me glance down below the side of Teassa's hull, and I became aware of the most enchanting fish that I had ever seen in my life gliding beneath me in the shadow of the boat. I caught my breath, for it was so stunning. It was like the king of fishes if there ever was one. It appeared to be straight out of the fairy tales of the world. In length it was some three to four feet and had a high protuberance on its head that looked exactly like a golden crown. His languid, sinuous body was of an exquisite, rich, scintillating depth of cobalt blue, shining through the sparkling, iridescent sea flowing towards his gently undulating double-pointed, golden vertical tail. The gold was of an unimaginable brightness and richness of hue, and all the colours were indescribably enhanced when caught in the light of the sun streaming through the water while it swam alongside. I truly could hardly believe my eyes and wondered how long he had he been there. But then, as in a dream, he drew away and was gone.

Because I was so frustrated with how the canvas sides to the cockpit had hampered my view, I took them down in case my visitor should return or some other wonder emerge from the depths. It was this fleeting visit that made me conscious of the wealth of life hidden in the oceans, as in the seas of my own unconscious life of soul. What a hidden treasure trove it was, filled with priceless forms of life!

On the morning of January 28th, the trade winds blew on average at force four and finally matched up to all my dreams and expectations, offering almost perfect sailing conditions and leaving me in no more doubt about completing my voyage. I benefited from its healing effects as I had originally hoped and anticipated before the voyage became a reality, and I felt more like my old self ten years before, just prior to Trevor in Cornwall writing the 'Spear of Destiny'. Indeed, I had felt like a wire stretched to breaking point by the time that I set sail on my voyage.

I put my fishing line out once more to try my luck, and quickly felt a pull and a tug. I drew the line in carefully towards the stern and pulled towards me a small golden fish with a rich blue spine. I carefully drew it over the side of the boat and onto the white wood-slatted cockpit seat next to the green hull. In a trice the golden colour withdrew in patches as the fish adapted to the varied colours of its surroundings, as did the sheen of mother of pearl. It gasped for the want of water, so quickly and with a feeling of reverent wonder, I picked up the fish, noticing as I removed the hook, that its body scales caught the rays of the sun in the blue sky and reflected ever more beautiful nuances of colour. I could do nothing other than return the fish to the sea as quickly as possible. There was nothing in life to which I could compare the experience. The memory of the exquisite, shimmering, sparkling and iridescent colours penetrated deep within my soul and awoke in me a new sense of wonder for the world that we live in.

January 29th provided a grey morning and Trade winds blowing at force three. No compass or sail changes were needed, just adjustments to the sheets and halyards. My accompanying fishes busily swam behind the stern and my bird flew in silent greeting, wings outspread to catch invisible air thermals as it circled effortlessly overhead, but unfortunately so high above the mast that I could not identify what sort of sea bird it was that had befriended me. The feathers appeared dark, possibly black. I liked to think that it was an albatross.

While reading and resting in the cockpit during the early afternoon, to my great joy, I again caught sight of the gold and blues of my previous visitor shimmering and sparkling through the sun-filled waves. He seemed to almost stop swimming as he slowly glided along with us for some half an hour. It was as if he was trying to convey something to me or allow something to be conveyed through his presence. It was magical!

I was entranced and time stood still as we inwardly communed with each other.

As he drew forward, I was able to observe that he was not alone but followed by another slightly smaller entirely blue fish, perhaps his fairy-tale queen. For me it was a deeply meaningful encounter, filling my soul with delight and comfort. Once more I felt reassured that I really was not alone. I felt a profound sense of inner warmth pervading my being and experienced an intimate oneness with the depths of the ocean and the heights of the surrounding heavens.

I recalled, while eating my supper of thick nutritious soup, a conversation I had with an American yachtsman in Tenerife who lived permanently on his boat with his wife. I had become despondent and disillusioned with my voyage, for it had not met my expectations. I had spent too much time with fear-ridden experiences rather than enjoying the sail. He had laughed, and said, 'Wait until you have experienced the Trades and then come and tell me how you feel!' Well I had finally come to understand exactly what he meant.

I became very disheartened however on the morning of January 30th, for the wind had slackened and I feared losing it altogether. Depression assailed me and I became aware that my body was complaining about the uncomfortable movement of the boat while on a broad reach across a drift current that had been created by the combination of the wind and the rotation of the earth. It prevented the possibility of complete relaxation and sound sleep on the sole, my bunk then being useless. My stomach was squashed, due to my sitting position, where my feet were jammed up against the opposite seat and my back against the sides of the cockpit in order to balance my body. My back was sore also and I did not have the luxury of being able to stand upright in the cabin, assuming that I was able to hang onto the handrails on the ceiling, because it was not high enough. Experiencing such conditions made me welcome the prospect of reaching Terra Firma where I could stand upright on firm and solid ground.

Homesickness descended upon me and I felt that I had had quite enough of sailing. I then realized that I needed to break this mood through action and so reluctantly decided to fish again, for I needed a change of diet. My heart was not in the task though and the line became horrendously entangled with the spinning line of the log's propeller streaming out to

116

stern. It took me ages to painstakingly untangle the two lines, but I was finally relieved to persuade myself that fishing was not a good idea unless there was no other alternative for survival.

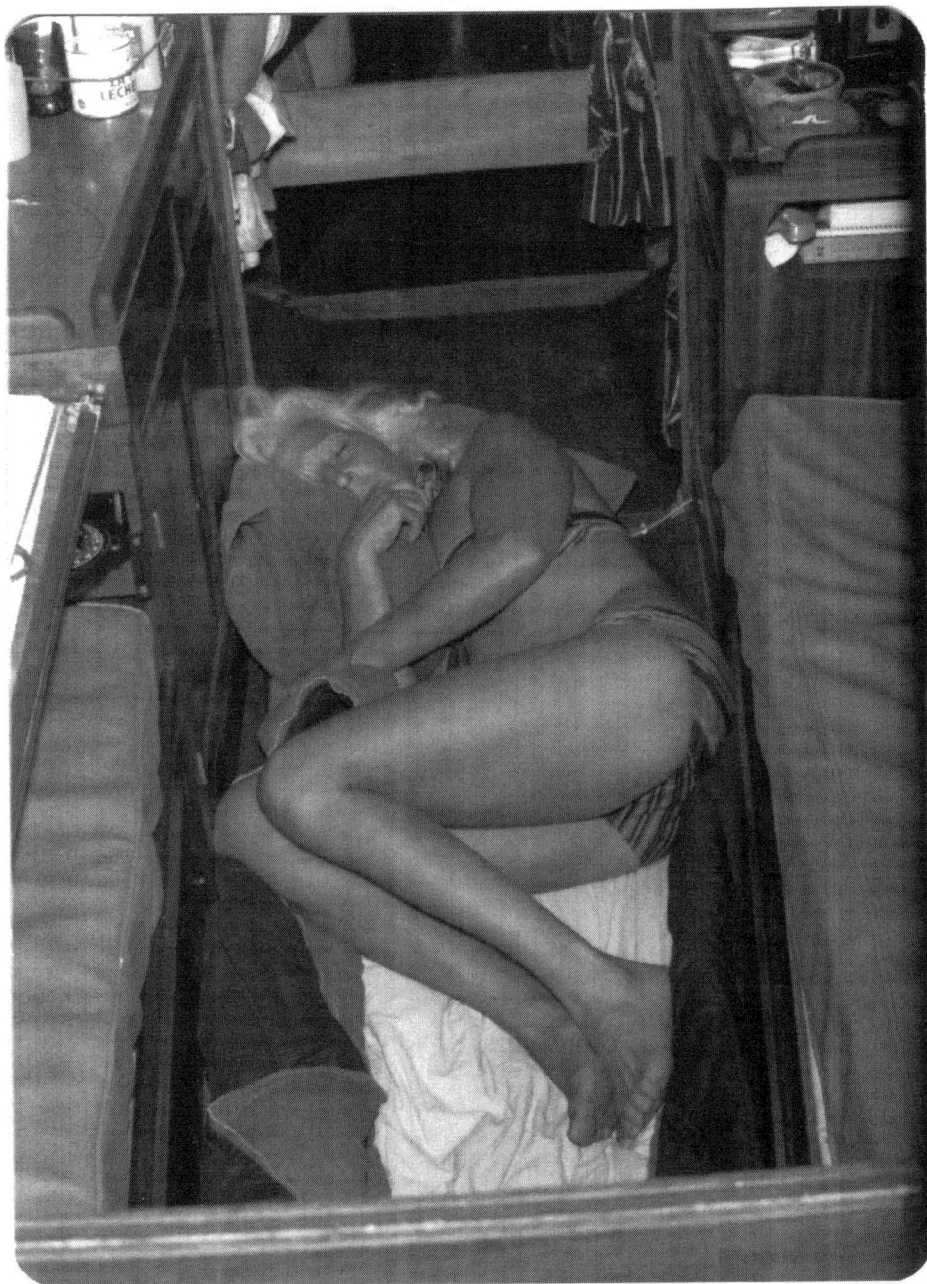

Lying on the sole of the boat

At noon I managed a first class sight, which matched up perfectly with my DR. I then decided that my depressed mood was unacceptable and that I had to throw it off somehow. Every adventure had to hit low spots and I just happened to be in one then.

Looking at my track across the chart, I calculated that I had sailed nearly another 1,000 miles and that if the wind held then I would be three quarters of the way across the Atlantic in three to four days. Then it suddenly occurred to me to check my radio to see if it was receiving anything from the approaching shores. Up to that point I had declined to use it for anything except navigation and lights, so as to conserve my batteries.

To my great joy and surprise, I could faintly hear pop music from the West Indies! That human contact cheered me up enormously and gave the incentive to treat myself at the prospect of nearing the end of my voyage. I ferreted out my dwindling supply of shampoo and hair conditioner and washed my hair with a limited amount of fresh though brackish tap water in the sink. I suspected that during my capsize sea water had got into the compartment where it was stored. Anyhow I was confident that I had plenty of bottled water stored in the bow for the remainder of my voyage. The shampoo was heavenly and so deliciously refreshing! Seawater had always made my hair feel terribly tacky. Using the remainder of the soapy water I washed my whole body and put on clean clothes. This felt absolutely wonderful!

As I dried my hair in the sun, the reality that I was so near to achieving my objective sank firmly into my consciousness. In response I made a hot drink and sat down in the cockpit to reminisce. The voyage up to this point had been an amazing experience, but not one that I would have liked to repeat. I was immensely grateful to have been given the opportunity to achieve my longed-for dream. It was finally becoming the cathartic experience, which I had envisioned and sought for as a basis for the future years of my life. Even then I did not feel like the same person that I was when I left Dartmouth, and I could foresee important changes ahead in my life, although I could not define them at this time. I knew though that it would take time to adjust to my new inward-developing awareness of self, with the consequent alterations in my life after my return.

Shirley using the boat's radio

The wind remained steady in between force four and five during the day of January 31st. We sailed under every stitch of canvas that I could put up. It was a beautiful sunny day, with scattered white clouds sweeping across the far distant skyline and being faithfully reflected in the white-topped glorious blue of the waves, rolling endlessly from horizon to horizon in one great stretch of ocean. I realized that I might not need to change the sails until I reached the West Indies and felt absolutely blissful at the prospect of a safe arrival after all my terrors and fearful experiences during the past weeks. I also realized that it would be Spring when I arrived home and that my cottage would be surrounded by woodland bursting into leaf and resplendent with wild primroses and daffodils and resounding with the song of birds establishing territories and building nests. What a heaven this would be.

When I looked into the sky I was wildly excited to see my first land-based seagull. It was circling overhead on the thermals, a black line penciled behind the eyes and a long slim pheasant-like tail trailing behind. I was jubilant, for this really was a sure sign that land was not far distant.

Adjusting the cover to the cabin entrance

After consulting the limited information that I had concerning the islands of the West Indies and my own direction, I decided to drop slightly south and set my course for Barbados, which was the nearest island. It had the essential advantage of an open, natural harbour, making it easier to sail into without the help of an engine. Then glancing out to port I was astonished to see, far away in the north-west, a large cruising vessel. This was my first sighting in thirty days, and only a single day from the three-quarter mark on my chart.

During the last days of my voyage, with no changes of sail or course, I had plenty of time to daydream. In fact the combination of the rolling motion of the boat with its familiar rhythmical sounds, and the fresh salty wind and health-giving warmth of the sun and sea, made me excessively dreamy and sleepy. I found that it became quite an effort to do anything constructive. The communal language of the living earth and the surrounding universe flowed into my inner being through all my senses throughout the days and nights and fired my imagination. I began to have an artistic comprehension of the joy, comfort and love that was drawn from my heart by the presence of my feathered companion. The whole kingdom of birds had always drawn from my heart feelings of joy, comfort and love ever since I was a child. To me a bird was an airy being, participating in the varying degrees of warmth in the air in which it lived, and which facilitated its effortless flight. It was a miniature earthly replica of what existed spiritually in higher realms: a transformed copy of an angelic being, a metamorphosed memory of a spiritual form. This, I thought, was what the great religious artists in the past had experienced naturally with capacities we today have lost. They seemed able to express in their works, in human dimensions, the influence of winged angelic beings within our earthly world, which accompanied and helped mankind down the ages.

My intensely vibrant full-bodied blue fish continued to visit me, swimming along on the port side in the shade, sharing a mutual communion. Like my heavenly feathered friend above, my ten or so small companions also followed faithfully behind, busily coming and going at will. These experiences helped me to understand that though the fish is an earthly being comprised of the moist elements of the earth, it is also an etheric creature participating in the life and cosmic breath of the earth: feeling at one with the exhaling life forces streaming out into the cosmos in spring and with the withdrawing life forces in winter. The exquisite colours of their bodily raiment, glittering through the waves, were to me an expression of their impregnation by stellar forces streaming from the cosmos.

On February 1st the wind was force five to six and the lumpy sea caused Teassa to leap and twist so excessively and awkwardly that I wondered whether I needed to reduce sail, but I decided not to because we were making splendid headway. It was another lovely sunny day with expressive white clouds flowing above the surrounding horizon and the cooling trade wind blew steadily behind, as I caught a glimpse of my small dark flying companion on one of his customary early morning visits. All seemed to be going well, but when I climbed onto the cabin roof to take my noon sight, I somehow let my only decent all-purpose bath towel slide off the roof and slip over the side of the boat into the sea. I had to watch it sink as it was swept away in the fast flowing water. This caused me to literally burst into floods of tears and I unashamedly howled my head off in sheer frustration at my loss. This made me realize what an oversensitive state I had worked myself into. After all, it was only a towel and not myself! I then accepted that I would have to be extra careful and also take hold upon myself. This voyage was proving to be an ultimate endurance test mentally, physically and spiritually, and I still had the final leg to complete.

During the sunshine and clouds of February 2nd I grasped what a blessing regular sleep was, particularly when your senses are bombarded day and night as they were in my circumstances. With the body in a constant state of movement, a conscious sense of balance is required for twenty-four hours each day. Under such conditions you began to feel like a prisoner in your body because your spirit and soul are unable to escape for respite and renewal into the unconscious night of the spiritual world. In fact I felt like a seemingly sleeping cat, with one eye slightly open, ear twitching, tail flicking and fear lurking in the guts. My faculties were tuned-in to danger and emergency and ready for instant action if needed. I was actually surprised how I had managed to maintain my daily life under such circumstances although I was aware of an enhanced state of sensitivity and a delicate emotional balance, along with an accompanying out-of-body state: an expansion of the soul into my environment and a feeling of inner oneness with the universe. However it was astonishing how restorative a short sleep proved to be.

On February 3rd I calculated that we had been averaging between eighty and ninety miles every twenty-four hours, which made me realize what an incredible difference it would have made if the trade winds had been with us all the way. The morning was as beautiful as ever and the kindly sun-filled trade wind blew us steadily and certainly towards our destination, the end of my adventure and dream.

I anticipated picking up a beacon from the West Indies and tried to imagine making harbour and contacting home. Then would have come the inevitable sale of Teassa to recover the money that Trevor had lent me to buy and equip her, and my return to England, Gallant's Bower in Dartmouth, and a very uncertain future since I never knew what Trevor had in mind even when I thought that I did. I wondered sometimes if he knew himself. For when things went well and all the balls were up in the air, he wanted to escape from family life, but when they were down he returned knowing that I could manage to survive on the smell of an oil rag, and then he could start writing his next book.

One thing that I would miss terribly was my much-loved Volkswagen, which I had to part with to help fund the purchase of my boat and equipment, and I also wondered how I was going to get Eve to her school in Dartington Hall every day. Such thoughts filled me with such an intense longing to reach that moment when I could drop anchor and contact my family to pick up the threads of my life again.

Sadly though, since I began to drop south, I seemed to have lost my travelling companions. Certainly there seemed to be no sign of them. Perhaps it was due to the approaching West Indies and consequential changes in wind and current directions. I was really left to my own devices with little to do but think during the final days of the voyage.

I became acutely conscious of how empty my human world would become without the members of my family, and how much the family had meant to me over the years, however hard the going became. How graced we were in the early years with a boundless wealth of love bonding us together, which was often remarked upon. But, with the exception of Eve, I could see that everyone had inevitably, and perhaps irretrievably, flown the nest in search of their own personal destiny. Our brief farewell gathering in Gallant's Bower, prior to my departure, was perhaps a conclusion in itself. But I realized that I had personally changed, having freed myself from the consciousness of the collective that held me prisoner. For the first time I felt myself to be a free spirit. A different scenario would inevitably unfold in my life and reveal itself after my return. I had found a new sense of ego, of my individual self, through orientating myself, under extreme pressure, alone without assistance and at the mercy of the elements for an extended length of time. Through this experience I had gained a great deal of confidence in myself.

On February 4th we sailed past the three-quarter mark on my track across the chart, so there was only about another 675 miles to pass under the keel before reaching Barbados.

As my gallant boat sailed on and on through time though I realized how much I would miss her in the years ahead! Yet the unfolding days and nights seemed endless, with no sail or course changes necessary and nothing to see but sea and sky. My spirit felt fulfilled but my aching body was tired and needed respite and my heart and soul yearned for the familiarity of home in spite of the prediction in Tenerife that the trade winds would yield the best days of the whole voyage. Certainly these winds possessed a particular quality of their own: a steady gentleness laced with sunshine and enfolded in the sympathy of all the elements in communion with one another. This altogether created a dreamlike sense of timelessness, peace and harmony, which completely pervaded the life of my soul, calming the restlessness of my searching spirit and calling me to wonder at the glories of creation, of which I was an integral part. I very much had the feeling of being a representative of the whole of humanity, just like a drop of water in relation to the oceans of the world. The symphony of the resounding universe intimated to me how Archetypal Man is a mirror of the Universe and how all that is arrayed before him is within. So, as the sun was the centre of the universe, of our solar system, according to Copernicus, my heart was felt to be the centre of my being, the cradle that awaited the birth of the spirit faculty in the life of my soul. Such a birth would awaken consciousness of the presence of God within.

With the arrival of February 5th, I had not had a decent noon sight for four days because of the sea conditions creating swells that prevented a view of a straight horizon. In addition my sight notebook had slipped away into the sea while I had balanced on the coach roof with my sextant. This was most unfortunate so close to the end of the voyage and made me aware that I had been getting careless.

I was pleased with the force six wind and, in this pleasant frame of mind, checked my general condition. My body was strong and slim since all excess fat had dropped conveniently off. It was also brown as a berry and full of sunshine and sea air. My hair was far too long and in urgent need of a haircut. But apart from that and fatigue, and general discomfort from the uncomfortable motion of the boat, with the resultant lack of sleep, I felt as fit as a fiddle. My supplies were still plentiful and Teassa was in an excellent condition taking into account all the general wear and tear. I needed, however, to strengthen and re-line some deck fittings, and give Teassa a good clean up and add a lick of paint and varnish here and there, and then have the engine checked. With the awareness of my voyage drawing to its conclusion, I begin tidying everything up and preparing for landfall.

I was thrilled to pieces during the morning of February 6th because I picked up the Antigua radio beacon. The day was cloudy, with slight rainfall, and we hurtled along in the strong force five to six winds, which unnerved me in my fragile state of mind. But I thought that it could not be more than three days to landfall. It was going to be such a delight to hear the Barbados beacon. It would be like sweet music to my ears! The thought of a proper night's sleep and nothing to worry about also seemed an attractive prospect.

I obtained a fairly reliable noon sight and that, in combination with the morning beacon, gave our position as approximately 300 miles from the island of Barbados. The old worries of making a landfall arose before me once more. Also I really did not like the long dark nights with poor visibility. But I could hardly believe that I was so close to the end of my voyage. I became filled with admiration for those who were able to just keep on and on until they had sailed around the world non-stop. I had finally come to realize that it was an incredible feat, demanding skills far beyond my own abilities, which I had experienced as being inadequate.

On February 7th, with the wind between force four and five, I could hear beacons but they were unidentifiable. I made an early breakfast and watched the sun rise from the grave of the night to reveal the world. The new day gradually became warm and sunny, with a clear blue sky over endless sweeps of water. I recalled having read somewhere that the Egyptians considered the world to be the self-expression of God and that the sacred word of its primal creator whispered through it, and that every human being was a word that God Himself had spoken. It was a wonderful thought to contemplate in this situation out on the ocean.

When I hauled up my washing-up water over the side of the boat, the excessive motion made it slosh around everywhere, including over myself. It was extraordinarily difficult washing-up in the bucket, for water got everywhere, and pots and pans ran uncontrollably around my feet.

Well that at least provided the opportunity to scrub the floor and surrounding cockpit!

During the evening the wind increased to between force five to six and the movement of the boat became so fast and uncontrollable that I reduced the sail area to facilitate a more pleasant night. I made the decision to sleep once more on the sole of the boat during the long hours of darkness.

As I watched the sun set and inhaled the breath of the open sea, a feeling of sadness clutched at my heart. I tried to warm myself with a hot mug of horlicks, and contemplated the magnificence and manifoldness of the starry heavens – a gigantic world of rhythms. Seen from my boat the whole firmament appeared to be revolving around its heavenly axis every twenty-four hours, giving the rhythm of day and night. (However I knew that modern astronomy stated that such rhythms were brought about by the daily rotation of the earth around its axis.)

There was the rhythm of the moon with its phases from new moon to full moon and back to new moon roughly within a month, and the rhythm according to modern astronomy where the earth moved around the sun during one year while we on earth perceived the sun in different parts of the sky. Then there was the rhythm of the seasons, arising from that circular movement of our earth around the sun. I felt that it was unfortunate that the modern mind regarded the firmament as an enormous mechanism and calculated its movements by applying purely mechanical laws, apparently overlooking the fact that a mechanism cannot create itself. If it could, then it would no longer be a mechanism. To me mechanisms were created by the human mind. In fact I earnestly desired to ask a scientist how the universe gained its motion. Such were the thoughts that occupied me as we slowly approached Barbados.

The wind dropped back to force four on February 8th but it was another glorious day. After breakfast I propped myself up in the shelter of the cabin and thought about myself with regard to the future. I wondered how I was personally going to bring order into my chaotic life in view of the unique and wonderful harmony and order that I experienced within the framework of the universe, and how was I going to bring a similar harmonious balance into the life of my soul and spirit. It all presented an enigma that I was incapable of solving at that point. I would have to wait to see how events would unfold. But in the mean time I had to prepare myself for crossing the new threshold back into the world of everyday

126

life. It was going to be a terrible shock and test and I had no means of knowing whether I would be able to manage it.

During the afternoon I received the longed-for faint sound of the Barbados beacon. It was one of the most poignant moments in my life. I cried out aloud with a hysterical sense of relief, letting go of a flood of pent up emotions, doubts, and feelings of anxiety.

In the dark early morning of February 9th, as I lay on the sole of my boat while she sailed over the glittering and sparkling sea, under a brilliant starry sky, I experienced for the first time in months a wonderful feeling of peace entering my soul. I realized that by next day I would have finally accomplished my dream.

The Barbados beacon was loud and clear throughout the day. With that bearing, a good sight, and my position established, I was then certain that I would arrive the following day. Knowing this, I literally fell on my knees with an intense sense of gratitude, and gave thanks.

The sky was alive with graceful tropical birds and grey-speckled seagulls, and Teassa's sails were well bellied-out by the wind. She confidently sliced her way through the white crests of waves that broke upon a sea as blue as lapis lazuli.

1 spent much of the rest of the day preparing for our fast approaching landfall. 1 fetched out my anchor from its quarters among the bags of sails, attached it to the anchor chain in the bow and then laid it ready to use on the deck. I stowed the tarpaulin, bagged any clothing that I no longer needed, and hung up garments that I thought I would need. Then I tidied up all my shelves and cupboards along with the things stowed in the bow. By evening everything was well prepared for our arrival next day. Then as I had plenty of fresh water left, I washed my hair and myself and my smalls. I then took bearings from three beacons at 23.00 hours. This revealed that I was forty-five miles from the island of Barbados and the Caribbean.

As Saturday 10th February 1980 dawned, I kept well off shore to avoid all hazards, and I observed shore lights in the early hours of the morning, but could see no visible navigational aids. Then, while the sun rose, low-lying land, which sloped gently to the edge of cliffs, came into view. I then made preparations to enter the well-sheltered Carlisle Bay, and sailed along the coast. I dismantled the spinnaker poles and secured them on deck, stowing lines, sheets and a genoa sail. I then used my remaining genoa and main sail for the remainder of my voyage.

Clearing South Point, I changed tack to enter Carlyle Bay off Bridgetown, the capital of Barbados. Deep pangs of regret filled my soul as I bade farewell to the ocean, which had given so much to me, from an unforgettable taste of the depths of hell to the dizzying heights of heaven.

Landing at Barbados

I dowsed my main sail and secured it to the boom with ties. Then, using my genoa to ghost past other boats at anchorage to reach the spot that I had chosen to anchor in, I quickly released the genoa halyard, dropped the sail on the deck, and threw my anchor into the sea.

Arrival – Barbados

Teassa drew astern until the chain ran its full length and the anchor held on the seabed four fathoms below. It was then 15.30 by my chronometer. I had sailed some 2,720 miles from Tenerife, spent forty days and nights at sea, and drawn dream and reality together in moments of rapture and imminent death on my quest to find deeper dimensions in the life of my soul. A heavenly peace descended as we rocked gently to the light swell in the bay, soothed by the rhythmically beating surf on that sandy shore-line fringed with palm trees.

Considering my life as a whole, it seemed a fitting end for a new beginning.

ELEVEN   Rejoicing, Anticlimax, Birth of Resolution

It was incredible to realize that I had accomplished the adventure of a lifetime, but soon 'reality' crashed back into my world. My dreamy reverie was shattered by a loud voice calling urgently through a megaphone: 'Are you the Granny who went to sea?'

Pulling myself together I stood up and looked around. The voice came from a magnificent aluminium Dutch racing yacht anchored to port. Wondering what this rude awakening was about I shouted, 'Yes, I guess I am! Why?'

'We have just heard over the radio that there's a lookout for you. Would you like to come and ring home on our ship-to-shore radio?'

Thinking what a generous offer this was I answered in the affirmative and excitedly climbed up towards the bows to unleash my Avon dinghy. As I inflated it, I prepared myself for my first encounter with fellow human beings after forty days and nights alone at sea.

Ensuing events proved to be a cruel and mundane end to this fateful and most important episode in my life. As I write, the memory draws unshed tears from my heart.

Ringing home, I was instructed not to talk to anyone, namely the media, until Trevor arrived with Tristan from New York three days later.

Meanwhile I was entertained royally over the weekend by my benefactors on the Dutch yacht who wanted to know all about the voyage. I then cleared customs and immigration on the following Monday in time to disembark. I was then able to join Trevor and Tristan in a holiday inn close to a white sandy beach lined with palm trees. Of course I was glad to see them and be taken care of but I felt that I was just a commodity to be sold, and Trevor behaved as if it was he himself who had undertaken the voyage. This was quite extraordinary when I think about it. I tried hard to co-operate though. I gave my charts, extra food and bottled water to a fellow yachtsman whom I had previously met in Tenerife, I stuffed my personal possessions into a kit bag and now the time had come to bid farewell to Teassa forever. To be fair though I had always known she could never be mine, yet the pain of the wrench from her lives with me to this day, for I was never to sail again.

I was not in a normal state of mind during the following days even though I went through the motions of everyday life. I was elated and in a heightened state of consciousness – even negotiating land was something that I had to adjust to. Perhaps this was delayed shock. Certainly I took advantage of the holiday setting and enjoyed tasty meals and cool drinks. I also had my long hair cut, did some shopping and endured an unreal interview by an American journalist supervised by Trevor. He represented a syndicate to whom Trevor had sold exclusive rights for my story and for which Trevor received some five thousand pounds, a considerable sum in those days.

During the following days while negotiations were taking place to sell Teassa lock stock and barrel, I tried, somewhat helplessly to prepare myself for the next chapter in my life; yet here I was relaxing in lonely isolation in the sun on a white sandy beach and swimming in the warm transparent sea.

I was later told that after the boat was beached for inspection, her engine once cleared of water, worked perfectly. Then I recollected miserably how that I could not even keep my much loved and precious sextant, which had been one of my prized possessions.

Relentlessly the days passed and within two weeks of reaching Barbados a doctor purchased Teassa and we were free to leave. I was very relieved when Trevor intimated he had recovered all the money that he had loaned me for the fitting out and purchase of the boat. We packed and flew to New York, then in the grip of snow and ice, and eventually to London. There we picked up Trevor's Volvo and drove to Devon.

We received a rapturous welcome from my daughters when we reached Gallant's Bower. Eve flew into my welcoming arms and cuddled up to me in deep relief and also during the following night in my big double bed. She also stayed close by throughout the following days. I needed her as much as she needed me, dearest, dearest Eve.

After some local media response, newspapers and TV set up by Trevor, I was forced, exhausted beyond measure by this time, to return post haste to London with him to discuss an agreement he had made with a publisher combining his own work and future deals and a book which he would put together with me regarding my voyage, titled 'The Ocean is My Adventure', subtitled 'Granny goes to Sea – a voyage to self-knowledge'. At some point Trevor received a down payment of a thousand pounds for this. Then after this I was duly packed off home to pick up the pieces of the life that I had left behind when I set out on my voyage just five months earlier.

Left to right: Michel, Eve, Shirley, Trevor

THE END

FOR A NEW BEGINNING

Postscript

While in one sense Trevor Ravenscroft, as husband and forceful personality, was the cause of Shirley's dependency, he also provided the key to unlock this door. The voyage which Trevor challenged Shirley to take had the effect of liberating her both from this dependency and allowed her to gain a sense of her own identity. The voyage in fact initiated a spiritual awakening – an awakening to her own self and individual purpose in the world.

The traumas of this Atlantic crossing and the experiences on the ocean over a period of several weeks also shocked Shirley into a deeper experience of her life as a biography therefore initiating this thirst for knowledge of her self and her personal destiny. This new direction gained from undertaking the voyage led Shirley to deep biographical study, which in turn formed itself into an idea of making a pilgrimage – but no ordinary pilgrimage: one made on horseback and taking in seven cathedrals on a route from Santiago de Compostela in Spain to Rosslyn Chapel in Scotland. With this journey Shirley attempted to experience the seven sites as stages in the development of a human biography and to interpret them as periods of development in the evolution of humanity. This, for Shirley, was another journey of discovery, but without the Atlantic crossing first, this would not have come to pass.

Trevor Ravenscroft may have provided the life-changing opportunity of the voyage but Shirley had to draw on her courage to embrace it as a means towards an initiatory transformation. Her courage shown in the face of fear comes as a much-needed example for us all today in facing the trials of the times we live in.

'Atlantic Threshold' is a foretaste of a work in progress in which Shirley tells her life story as a concrete demonstration of the principles of biographical development. When this is published it will smoothly complete what is here otherwise an eventful episode but with a rather abrupt cliff hanging ending.

WB